How to Get Published: 50 Successful Query Letters

By Brett Weiss

Publisher: Dark Dreamer Publishing
brettw105@sbcglobal.net
www.brettweisswords.com

ACKNOWLEDGEMENTS

Thanks to the many editors I've worked with over the years, including editors for *AntiqueWeek*, *Back Issue*, *Filmfax*, *Video Game Trader*, the *Fort Worth Star-Telegram*, McFarland Publishers, and Schiffer Publishing.

Thanks to James and Livia Reasoner, who are great interview subjects.

Thanks to Charis, Ryan, and Katie Weiss, who help keep me going.

Thanks to Mom, who let me play with her old typewriter, and to Dad, the very definition of a patriarch. We miss you, Dad.

How to Get Published: 50 Successful Query Letters

Table of Contents

Introduction

50 Query Letters that Led to Paying Jobs

Breakthrough

Anatomy of a Near Nervous Breakdown

How to Get Published

How Writing Can Supplement Your Income

Writers in Movies

The History of Typewriters

Interview with Author James Reasoner

Interview with Brett Weiss

How to Get Published: 50 Successful Query Letters

Introduction

With *How to Get Published: 50 Successful Query Letters*, you'll discover that most any reasonably intelligent person with a strong work ethic and a love for reading and writing can get published, at least from time to time and maybe even on a regular basis. There's no magic involved, but I do offer some tips and tricks you'll need to know in order to achieve success in the field of writing.

As the title suggests, this book focuses primarily on how to write query letters, but I provide other pointers along the way, along with an assortment of writing-related essays and articles near the back of the book.

Before I continue, let me give you a few of my qualifications so you know you aren't wasting your time. I'm a former writer and editor for the All Game Guide (allgame.com), and I'm the author of the *Classic Home Video Games* book series (McFarland Publishers) and of *The 100 Greatest Console Video Games: 1977-1987* (Schiffer Publishing).

I write comic book descriptions for mycomicshop.com, I was on the *Comics Buyer's Guide* Review Crew for more than a decade, and I'm a frequent contributor to a major metropolitan newspaper, the *Fort Worth Star-Telegram*, and a national newspaper, *AntiqueWeek*.

In addition, I've had articles published in *Alter Ego*, *The Auction Exchange & Collector's News*, *Back Issue*, *Classic Gamer Magazine*, *Fangoria*, *Farm World*, *Filmfax*, *Game Informer*, *Hogan's Alley*, *Indulge*, *Living with Panache*, *Mystery Scene*, *Native Peoples*, *Nevada Magazine*, the *PinGame Journal*, *Robot* magazine, *Scary Monsters*, *Toy Car & Model*, *Toy Shop*, *Treasures*, *Video Game Collector*, *Video Game Trader*, *The West Texan News*, *The Writer*, and *You & Me: America's Medical Magazine*.

In short, I write a lot, and the vast majority of it gets published.

A major key to my getting published so frequently is my ability to write a strong, concise query letter, which any successful writer must learn how to do, whether you want to pitch articles, stories, or book ideas.

What is a query letter, exactly? It can be a pitch to a literary agent, but for the purposes of this book it's a letter to a magazine editor or a publishing house, proposing an article or book idea. Of course, editors for newspapers and websites receive query letters as well. A good query letter is direct and to the point, letting the editor know what the article or book idea is about and why you are qualified to write it.

The queries in this book, all of which lead to sales, are real letters I wrote to real editors. Each letter is preceded by commentary in which I explain why it was successful in convincing the editor to accept my article or book idea.

Prior to digging in to the meat of this book—the query letters themselves—check out the following list of 10 tips for writing successful query letters as they will give you a good foundation going in. These tips won't guarantee that you'll get published—it's up to you to do the market research, the writing, and other legwork (fingerwork?)—but they will help give you a fighting chance.

1. Include your name, email address, and phone number at or near the top of the page, preferably on professional looking letterhead.
2. Unless you have worked with the editor many times before or know him or her personally, address him or her as "Mr." or "Ms."
3. Never begin an article pitch with your publication credits or other information about yourself. Rather, go directly to your pitch and include your bio and credits near the end of the query.
4. Have another writer—one more established than you—read your query before you send it. If you don't know any other writers, you

need to get busy at once networking through social media and writing workshops.

5. Before pitching an idea to an editor of a magazine or newspaper, read at least two or three issues of the publication in question so you'll know what type of material they publish, in terms of both style and content. Prior to submitting a book idea, pour over that publisher's website or catalogue, making sure they publish the type of book you have in mind.

6. Don't ramble in your query letter—it should fit on a single page. Two to six well-written paragraphs are usually ideal.

7. Prior to writing a query letter, look over the publication's (or publisher's) submission guidelines to find out exactly what they are looking for and how they want you to send it. For example, certain markets won't accept email submissions while others won't open any email that contains an attachment.

8. Unless the editor requests it, steer clear of asking him or her to click on a link. However, feel free to include the link to your blog or website at the end of the pitch below your name.

9. Sell yourself without coming across as a snooty know-it-all. Near the end of the pitch, with your bio and relevant publishing credits, state in matter-of-fact fashion why you are the right person to write the book or article.

10. Read query letters that led to paying jobs. Fortunately for you, constant reader (and, hopefully, writer), there are 50 such query letters in the palm of your hand.

One note: You'll notice that a number of the queries in this book don't include my biographical info or credentials. That is only because when those particular queries were written, I already had a longstanding working relationship with those respective editors, and they were already well aware of my qualifications (despite this, I still had to write compelling queries or I wouldn't get work). If you are new to a publication or don't know the editor very well, you will always want to explain your qualifications.

Best of luck in your chosen profession—I sincerely hope that reading *How to Get Published: 50 Successful Query Letters* will help lead you to a happy and successful writing life.

~Brett Weiss
December 18, 2014

Query Subject: 8-Track Tapes
Publication: AntiqueWeek
Why this query worked: I touched on a timely, trendy topic, made it relevant to a newspaper about antiques, and promised to quote experts on the subject.

■■■

Brett Weiss
817 – XXX - XXXX
brettw105@sbcglobal.net

Dear [Mr. or Ms. _____]:

With the hoopla surrounding recorded music these days—the resurgence of LPs, the ubiquity of digital downloads, the decline of CDs, and the like—the time is right for an article about 8-track tapes, that much-maligned, but oftentimes fondly remembered music format.

Mention 8-Tracks to anyone over 40, and you'll likely get laughter and/or smiles in return. Whether loathed or loved, 8-track tapes are an interesting topic, especially for nostalgia enthusiasts. Also, while most 8-track tapes can be found for a buck or less, some are worth hundreds or even thousands of dollars.

I propose a feature on 8-tracks, with quotes by and photos of Kathy Gibson, owner of Kate's Track Shack, a respected online retailer that buys, sells, and repairs 8-track tapes, players, and accessories. They also transfer 8-tracks to CDs and CDs to 8-tracks. They even produce new 8-tracks for current bands, such as Cheap Trick's *The Latest*, which was featured on Stephen Colbert's TV show.

I will also include quotes from Bucks Burnett, who recently opened the world's first 8-track tape museum, which is located in Dallas, TX.

Please let me know if you are interested in such an article.

Thanks for your time!

Sincerely,

Brett Weiss

Query Subject: A New Book: The 100 Greatest Console Video Games: 1977-1987

Publisher: Schiffer Publishing

Why this query worked: I established the fact that a video game book like this had never been written before (and why one should be written), I gave examples of similar books in other fields, I said how I would promote the book, and I established my credentials on the subject.

■■■

Brett Weiss
817 – XXX - XXXX
brettw105@sbcglobal.net

Dear [Mr. or Ms. _____]:

While reading *Bill Warren's Keep Watching the Skies!: American Science Fiction Movies of the Fifties*, a book idea hit me over the head like the proverbial ton of bricks. My new book, *The 100 Greatest Console Video Games: 1977-1987*, will be the video game equivalent of Warren's sci-fi movie masterpiece, but instead of covering a particular genre, my book will feature the 100 best games from the era. (Other influences on my book include: *Horror: The 100 Best Books* by Stephen Jones and Kim Newman; *Fantasy: The 100 Best Books* by James Cawthorn and Michael Moorcock; *100 Greatest Comic Books* by Jerry Weist; and *The 100: A Ranking of the Most Influential Persons in History* by Michael H. Hart.)

For each of the 100 games, I will write 800-1,500 words of detailed, fun-to-read information, from storyline to gameplay to production history to critical commentary. In addition, I'll include statistical data, personal anecdotes, tips and tricks, quotes from reviews found in magazines and other books, quotes from programmers, memorabilia pricing, and more.

Numerous top 100 (and top 50 and top 200) video game lists have appeared in magazines and on websites over the years, but the text is typically brief and lacking in substance. In addition, the parameters are usually too loosely defined, with the writers including old, new, and somewhere-in-between arcade, computer, console, and handheld games. In short, no other video game book like this has ever been published.

The reasons I chose 1977-1987 as the era of coverage are many. The all-important Atari 2600 was released in 1977, the Atari 5200 and ColecoVision were released in 1982, and many of the most important titles in the Nintendo NES library, including *Castlevania*, *The Legend of Zelda*, *Super Mario Bros.*, and *Metroid*, hit stores in 1987. If I were to include 1988 (and beyond), many key titles from earlier years would have to be dropped. I like that the book will cover a single, highly influential decade in gaming.

Many of the games from this era, especially the ones my book will cover, are still being played via emulators, classics collections, downloads for current consoles, and eBay and video game convention acquisitions. In addition, many of the games in the book have spawned modern sequels and remakes, which I will mention. These and other factors make the book relevant today beyond pure nostalgia. The book is sure to generate robust discussions, with gamers arguing over which titles should and shouldn't have made the cut.

The 100 Greatest Console Video Games: 1977-1987 will be finished by July 30, 2013 and will be approximately 100,000 to 130,000 words in length. I will provide photos of game cartridges, game boxes, magazine ads, game programmers, memorabilia, and more, with each game getting four photos.

Thanks for considering my book for publication. It will be much, much different from my *Classic Home Video Games* series (McFarland Publishers), which catalogues every classic game with short, encyclopedia-style entries, but fans of my books will surely be interested. I'm a busy self-promoter, posting links online, handing out fliers, setting up at shows (classic gaming expos are popping up all over the country), communicating with reviewers (for *Game Informer*, *Video Game Trader*, and other publications), and more, so

The 100 Greatest Console Video Games: 1977-1987 will receive plenty of exposure on my end.

In addition to the *Classic Home Video Games* series, I've had articles about video games published in *AntiqueWeek*, the *Fort Worth Star-Telegram*, *Game Informer*, *Toy Shop*, *Video Game Collector*, *Video Game Trader*, *Classic Gamer Magazine*, *The Atari 2600 Connection*, the *Comics Buyer's Guide*, *Nevada Magazine*, and the *PinGame Journal*.

I'm a former editor and writer for the All Game Guide (allgame.com), I've been a gamer since 1974, and I've written about video games professionally since the late 1990s.

If you are interested in this book idea, please contact me at your convenience. I'll be happy to discuss the project and provide sample chapters. I've attached images for your perusal.

Query Subject: Anatomy of a Near Nervous Breakdown
Publication: You & Me Medical Magazine
Why this query worked: I did the legwork on finding a suitable place to submit a very personal story. Plus, I think I did a pretty good job of playing up the semi-dramatic nature of what happened. As a writer, when something unusual happens to you in life, especially something bad, you should turn it into an article or essay.

■■■

Brett Weiss
817 – XXX - XXXX
brettw105@sbcglobal.net

Dear [Mr. or Ms. _____]:

A few months ago my health spiraled downward, and I had no idea why. I was experiencing heart palpitations, extreme anxiety, and severe nervousness, and I couldn't concentrate on anything beyond the mundane. In addition, I would get lightheaded any time I would stand up too quickly. Once I even fainted for a few seconds and fell on our family entertainment center. My job, which is freelance writing, became all but impossible during this time.

After consulting with a number of medical specialists, who ran EKGS, did blood tests, and hooked me up to a heart monitor, there was no answer in sight. I was scheduled to undergo further tests, including a brain scan, when one doctor—a neurologist—casually asked me how I had been sleeping. I told him not well. He asked if I drank a lot of coffee, tea, or soda, and I told him I have two or three cups of Earl Grey every morning when I write. The doctor told me to cut down on caffeine, but I quit it altogether, cold turkey.

Amazingly, within a day or so of quitting caffeine, all my symptoms disappeared. Today I feel great and only ingest caffeine in small amounts.

My article on the above experience will be dramatic (to a point) and humorous and will make for worthwhile reading. I'm thinking 800-1200 words will sum up what happened.

Please let me know if you are interested in such an article.

Query Subject: Atari 2600
Publication: AntiqueWeek
Why this query worked: Nostalgia for the Atari 2600 was booming when I pitched the article, and, while *AntiqueWeek* had rarely (if ever) published anything about video games in the past, the increasing auction prices for the console and some of its rarer games made it a relevant topic. I wrote the query in such a way that even a non-gamer would understand the importance of the Atari 2600.

■■■

Brett Weiss
817 – XXX - XXXX
brettw105@sbcglobal.net

Dear [Mr. or Ms. _____]:

Released in 1977, the original Atari 2600 is more than a simple video game system—it's a pop culture touchstone. To many in their late 30s through their 50s and beyond, the word "Atari" is synonymous with "video game."

During its 14-year lifespan, the Atari 2600 sold nearly 30 million units, along with hundreds of millions of cartridges, including such hits as *Ms. Pac-Man*, *Missile Command*, and *Space Invaders*. Today, the system is much more than an outdated piece of electronics history. Thousands of gamers and nostalgia buffs are hooking vintage Atari consoles to their television sets, rediscovering the past in a fun, interactive manner.

Moreover, some of the rarer Atari 2600 games—especially those complete in the original packaging—sell for hundreds and in some cases thousands of dollars. Also, certain enterprising programmers are creating new cartridges for the beloved system and selling them online and at trade shows, complete with professionally produced boxes and manuals.

I propose an article on the Atari 2600: the history, the nostalgia, the collectability, the resurgence. I can provide photos and collector quotes, and I'll ensure that the article will appeal to a broad base.

Please let me know if you are interested in such an article.

Query Subject: Bentley Little Interview
Publication: Fangoria
Why this query worked: Since *Fangoria* is a specialty horror magazine, I had a good interview subject, who I tracked down online before I even had a publisher for a prospective article. In the query I got straight to the point, pointing out (so to speak) the importance of Bentley Little to the field of horror fiction.

■■■

Brett Weiss
817 – XXX - XXXX
brettw105@sbcglobal.net

Dear [Mr. or Ms. _____]:

Are you interested in an interview with Bentley Little?

Here's a brief bio on Mr. Little:

Born in Mesa, Arizona in 1960, a month after his mother attended the world premiere of *Psycho*, Bentley Little is a horror novelist supreme, garnering effusive praise from such luminaries in the field as Stephen King and Dean Koontz. In fact, when King was hit by a van and almost killed in 1999, *USA Today* reported that he was holding a copy of Little's *The House*. Like King, Little typically writes un-abstruse prose about scary supernatural happenings in small towns.

In 1990, Little was awarded the Bram Stoker Award for "Best First Novel for The Revelation." In 1993, *The Summoning* was a Bram Stoker Award nominee. Throughout the 1990s and up until today (he's busy on a novel, but doesn't like to talk about current works in progress), Little has been a steady craftsman, cranking out at least one novel in most years. His latest, *The Disappearance*, which is about a missing girl, was published in 2010.

I've been reading mainstream, literary, and horror fiction for more than 30 years, and I've had articles published in numerous magazines, including *The Writer*, *AntiqueWeek*, *Filmfax*, *Robot*, *Farm World*, and the *Comics Buyer's Guide*. I also freelance for the *Fort Worth Star-Telegram*, and I'm the author of the *Classic Home Video Games* book series.

If you are interested in an article on and interview with Bentley Little, please let me know.

Query Subject: The Brady Bunch
Publication: AntiqueWeek
Why this query worked: Most everyone who grew up during the
1970s has fond memories of *The Brady Bunch*, and the show is still
super popular. *AntiqueWeek*, which has a large, broad-based
readership, publishes a fair amount of articles about vintage pop
culture collectibles, so my idea was a good fit. Plus, having
interviewed someone who runs a prominent *Brady Bunch* website
certainly didn't hurt.

■ ■

Brett Weiss
817 – XXX - XXXX
brettw105@sbcglobal.net

Dear [Mr. or Ms. _____]:

Created by Sherwood Schwartz, who also helmed *Gilligan's Island*,
The Brady Bunch aired on ABC from 1969 to 1974 and was
cancelled after five seasons. Although it wasn't a ratings bonanza for
the network (the show never cracked Nielson's top 25 during the
five years it aired), *The Brady Bunch* found its true audience in
syndication. *Brady Bunch* reruns began airing in September of 1975
(frequently in the afternoon and early evening, when kids are home
from school), and since that time the show has never been off the air,
resulting in millions of fans worldwide.

One of the most beloved television programs ever filmed, *The Brady
Bunch* is still frequently referenced in books, movies, magazines,
speeches, articles, everyday conversations, and other TV shows.
The program, which is in constant syndication, represents an ideal
view of the American family, and people take comfort in watching
it.

How about a feature on America's favorite fictional family? My
article would cover the show's history, cultural impact, fans, and
collectibles, and it would include quotes from collectors, including

Wendy Winans, a huge *Brady Bunch* fan who runs www.bradyworld.com.

Query Subject: Breakthrough as a Writer
Publication: The Writer
Why this query worked: The editor for *The Writer* preferred long queries detailing what would be useful to their readership, which was largely comprised of aspiring writers, so that's what I wrote. It helped that I had a compelling story with a 9/11 tie-in.

■ ■

Brett Weiss
817 – XXX - XXXX
brettw105@sbcglobal.net

Dear [Mr. or Ms. _____]:

I'm convinced my story on how I "broke through" to publication would make for interesting reading. Back in 2006, I attended Comic-Con International in San Diego, introduced myself to an editor (business card in hand), and succeeded in corresponding with that editor over the course of the next few weeks (long enough to get a deal for a video game book series).

Prior to that, I had been working on a video game book for a different publisher, but that project was cancelled due to the economic downturn after 9/11. My article will describe how devastated I was after the cancellation of that first book to the elation I felt upon signing the new contract, and I would emphasize how important it is to make contacts within the industry.

Additional advice my article will provide:

*Wake up each morning a couple of hours before everyone else in the house, fix yourself a strong cup of coffee or hot tea, and get some writing in while you are fresh and the house is quiet.

*Keep an organized filing system containing publisher contacts and addresses, stories and articles written, rejection and acceptance notices, sample copies of various publications you are trying to "break into," and anything else related to your writing.

*Treat yourself like a professional. Call yourself a writer. Act like a writer. Carry a notebook with you, jotting down anything interesting someone might say or any story, article, or book idea that may pop into your head.

Lessons learned will include:

*Prior to submitting a book proposal to a publisher, read (or at least flip through) some of their books to get an idea of what type of material they publish. The same goes for articles and stories. If you haven't read the magazine in question, there's little chance your story or article will be published in that magazine. To cut down on the expenses of doing this, check your local library. Or, regarding magazines, send off for a sample copy or check out sample copies online.

*Don't get so excited about your book contract that you drop everything, including well-paying articles, to write it. If the publisher is agreeable to the time frame, allow yourself plenty of time to write the book and do your other writing. Moreover, take extra time on the book so you will cut down on mistakes. If you think the book will take a year to write, for example, allow for 16 months.

*Never throw away anything you have written, no matter how bad. That terrible short story you wrote 15 years ago could provide at least a skeleton of an idea for a terrific screenplay or comic book script.

Query Subject: Buddy Saunders
Publication: Alter Ego
Why this query worked: A comics retailer, fandom pioneer, and writer like Buddy Saunders is ideal fodder for *Alter Ego,* a publication that focuses on Golden and Silver Age comic books. I interviewed Buddy before I even got the gig, assuming they would probably be interested. I played up the fact that Buddy was a key figure in early comics fandom and is still involved in the industry today.

■■

Brett Weiss
817 – XXX - XXXX
brettw105@sbcglobal.net

Dear [Mr. or Ms. _____]:

Would you be interested in taking a look at a recent interview I conducted with Buddy Saunders? As you may well know, Buddy was active in early comic book fandom, publishing the groundbreaking *Star-Studded Comics* (as a member of the legendary Texas Trio), and he also contributed art and stories to other seminal fanzines. In addition, he wrote around 25 or so stories for Warren publications.

Buddy wrote prose fiction as well. His "Back to the Stone Age" was nominated for a Nebula in 1976, and he co-authored the paperback novel, *The Texas-Israeli War: 1999*. These days he owns a seven-store comic book chain in Texas, and he runs mycomicshop.com, one of the industry's largest online retailers.

Perhaps even more importantly, Buddy is getting ready to launch a new nationwide print publication featuring science fiction short stories. The new magazine is designed as a more traditional alternative to *Asimov's* and *Fantasy & Science Fiction.*

Please let me know if you are interested in taking at look at my interview with Mr. Saunders.

Query Subject: Chuck Rozanski: Collector of Native American Potter
Publication: Native Peoples Magazine
Why this query worked: Sometimes who you interview can be about as important as your skill as a writer, so try to talk to interesting people who do unusual things. This is certainly applies to Chuck Rozanksi, a fascinating spiritualist who has amassed an incredible collection of Native American pottery.

▪▪

Brett Weiss
817 – XXX - XXXX
brettw105@sbcglobal.net

Dear [Mr. or Ms. _____]:

Most hardcore specialty collectors are content to conquer a single field of collecting. This is definitely not the case with Chuck Rozanski, owner and president of Mile High Comics, one of the largest online comic book retailers in America. In addition to running Mile High Comics, which includes four brick-and-mortar stores in the Denver metro area, Rozanski is one of the world's foremost Pueblo pottery collectors, owning more than 8,500 pieces.

Rozanski is a passionate collector who feels spiritually connected to his collection, as well as to those who make the pottery. He even has body art commemorating his collection.

"I have had a remarkably large and beautiful Tewa-inspired prayer, which incorporates images from seven pieces of pottery by 1930's Pueblo artist Van Gutierrez, tattooed over my entire upper torso," he said. "As a direct result, thoughts of my pottery collection never leave me."

Are you interested in an article on Mr. Rozanski? I recently interviewed him, and he came through with some wonderful quotes. I can tailor the length of the prospective article to meet your needs.

I'm a full-time freelancer, and one of my jobs is to write collector/collection profiles for an assortment of publications, most notably cover features for *AntiqueWeek*.

Please let me know if you have any questions or would like to see some published clips.

Query Subject: Classic Gaming Expo
Publication: Nevada Magazine
Why this query worked: Timing and market research worked hand-in-hand to ensure that I had the right idea for the proper publication. Video game magazines don't typically run previews of video game conventions (they prefer post-con reports), so I Googled Nevada publications and found a mainstream magazine that publishes articles on local conventions of all kinds before they happen.

∙∙

Brett Weiss
817 – XXX - XXXX
brettw105@sbcglobal.net

Dear [Mr. or Ms. _____]:

A Las Vegas staple, the Classic Gaming Expo enters its 13th year as the world's first and largest event paying tribute to the video games of yesteryear. The 2012 convention will feature vendors, guest speakers, live music, an auction, tournaments, author signings and more celebrating the rich history of video gaming, from Pong to PlayStation, from Atari to Xbox.

If you are interested in a story on the Classic Gaming Expo, which will be held Aug. 11-12 at The Plaza Hotel & Casino, please let me know. I've been to CGE several times before and have always had a wonderful time. It's a truly special event for nostalgia buffs, pop culture enthusiasts, casual players, hardcore gamers, families and anyone else looking to have a good time.

I'm a full-time freelancer, writing for the *Fort Worth Star-Telegram*, *AntiqueWeek*, *Game Informer*, *The Writer*, *Mystery Scene*, and numerous other publications. I'm also the author of the *Classic Home Video Games* book series (McFarland Publishers). If you would like to see clips, I'll be happy to send them.

Query Subject: New Book: Classic Home Video Games, 1972-1984
Publisher: McFarland Publishers
Why this query worked: When I attended Comic-Con International: San Diego in 2006, I spoke to an editor running McFarland Publishers' booth and gave her my business card, telling her to contact me if I could contribute to any of their forthcoming reference guides on movies, music, or other pop culture topics. Three days after I got home, she emailed me asking if I had any book ideas. Apparently, I did have a good idea—she said the pitch was a unanimous "yes" during the editorial meeting that followed. My query laid out a clear, detailed picture of what the book was going to be, and I illustrated that I was capable of writing such a book. As requested, I included a sample entry.

■■■

Brett Weiss
817 – XXX - XXXX
brettw105@sbcglobal.net

Dear [Mr. or Ms. _____]:

I've been looking for just the right publisher for a book idea that's been brewing in the back of my mind for a long time, and I believe McFarland, with its penchant for publishing encyclopedic entertainment books, would be just the right fit.

I realize that your company has never published a book about video games, but please bear with me a moment while I explain why I think my idea would be a good fit. My book would be a video game encyclopedia covering all U.S.-released, pre-Nintendo game systems and cartridges, meaning the years 1972-1984 would be covered. (Nintendo ushered in the era of modern home gaming, so there's a distinct cutoff point between the classics and the modern era.)

Each game for each system during these formative years of interactive entertainment would be given an entry. Each entry would offer a brief, but colorful description of the game, plus any pertinent historical information (or other interesting tidbit) about the game.

This book will be ambitious in scope, but very doable as I have plenty of games, personal experience, and reference materials to cover every game. Classic gaming is hugely popular among younger and older fans and is growing by the day. A volume of this type should prove to be a commercial success.

I've included an attachment with an example of what I have in mind (less important releases would have shorter entries). Please let me know if you have any questions or you would like to discuss my proposal further.

Query Subject: Comic Book Display
Publication: AntiqueWeek
Why this query worked: *AntiqueWeek* has a monthly column called "Insights," which provides insider information on a variety of topics related to the antique and collectibles market. My pitch offered a practical solution to a common problem among comic book fans. One thing that sold the editor on the idea was the fact that the display could be used by both collectors and retailers.

■■

Brett Weiss
817 – XXX - XXXX
brettw105@sbcglobal.net

Dear [Mr. or Ms. _____]:

For years, comic book dealers, including antique booth operators who sell comics, have struggled with finding a good way to display their back issues. Old comics take up a lot of room and are slow sellers compared to their new-on-the-shelf counterparts, but they can bring in nice profits over time, especially when displayed properly.

I recently opened a booth in an antique mall, and during this process, I've discovered a way to display comic books in lateral file cabinets. I saw such a display at a local comic book store. It's an easy, yet ingenious system where you remove some of the hardware from the filing cabinet, and store the comics in short boxes. Customers can open the file cabinet drawers to thumb through thousands of issues in an area that takes up relatively little space.

This type of altered filing cabinet would also work great as storage for comic book collectors.

Are you interested in an instructional article on how to convert a lateral filing cabinet into a comic book storage/display unit?

Query Subject: DC Comics' New 52
Publication: Fort Worth Star-Telegram
Why this query worked: DC Comics, publishers of such legendary characters as Batman and Superman, revamped its entire comic book line, a sure bet for an article aimed at the entertainment section of a family newspaper. I think I did a good job of describing the event concisely, but with enough detail to communicate my idea for the article.

■■■

Brett Weiss
817 – XXX - XXXX
brettw105@sbcglobal.net

Dear [Mr. or Ms. _____]:

DC Comics, publishers of such legendary heroes as Superman, Batman, and Wonder Woman, is turning the comic book industry upside down by rebooting its entire line. Beginning Aug. 31 and continuing through Sept. 28, the company is publishing 52 #1 issues, meaning all its long-running (and short-running, for that matter) titles are starting over. Pop culture fans everywhere are abuzz over this development.

I propose a story about this massive makeover, which is intended to bring new readers into the fold. My story will spotlight 15 of the more popular titles (Such as *Batman* #1, *Superman* #1, *The Flash* #1, and *Green Lantern* #1) and list all the rest in a sidebar. The story will give prospective comic book purchasers fun, easy-to-digest info (basic premise, creative team, etc.) on each spotlighted title.

Given the popularity of super-heroes these days, the story is sure to be a hit with readers of all ages.

Query Subject: Elvis Presley and Graceland
Publication: Treasures
Why this query worked: In the aftermath of our family trip to Graceland, I scoured the Internet, looking for a good fit for an article on Elvis and Graceland. I found *Treasures*, which my local library happened to carry, so I read a couple of issues, got a feel for the types of stories they like to publish, and pitched the article. As a bonus, I was able to write off part of the trip on my taxes.

■■

Brett Weiss
817 – XXX – XXXX
brettw105@sbcglobal.net

Dear [Mr. or Ms. _____]:

One of the most endearing and enduring pop culture icons of the last century, Elvis Presley was and is The King of Rock and Roll. In addition to a string of gold albums and number one hits, Elvis spawned a flood of merchandise, much of it rare and valuable today. Such items as billfolds, record cases, bubblegum cards, board games, and comic books now go for hundreds of dollars and in some cases thousands.

I've been a huge Elvis fan since I was a kid, and I've been to Graceland. And I'm very familiar with the collector's market surrounding Elvis, including items still being produced today.

Are you interested in an article on Elvis? I can provide photos and fascinating, fun-to-read information.

A full-time freelancer, I've had articles published in *AntiqueWeek*, *Fangoria*, *Filmfax*, *Toy Shop*, *Farm World*, the *Fort Worth Star-Telegram*, and numerous other publications.

Query Subject: The Flash
Publication: Back Issue
Why this query worked: As a lifelong fan of the Flash, I jumped on the chance to write about the character for *Back Issue* magazine. My query, which was a response to the editor sending out a request for pitches about the death of the Flash, was essentially an outline covering all the bases, from when he died to when he was brought back from the grave.

■■■

Brett Weiss
817 – XXX - XXXX
brettw105@sbcglobal.net

Dear [Mr. or Ms. _____]:

My article on the death of the Flash will provide a basic background for the character, the reasons behind DC and Marv Wolfman killing him off, how he was killed off (and what it accomplished), and how he was recently brought back.

The article would also cover how DC refused to bring Barry back for years, what the industry was like at the time of his death (people were actually surprised by his death during those pre-Internet days), and what it meant to fans of the era who mourned his death (I will quote fans and creators in this regard). In addition, I will comment on how the comics characters in the stories responded to his death and return.

Thanks for considering my pitch for an article on my all-time favorite super-hero!

Best,

Brett Weiss

P.S. My office is covered with Flash memorabilia, and I own every Flash comic book from #105 to the present.

Query Subject: Gay Marriage in Archie Comics
Publication: AntiqueWeek
Why this query worked: A socially relevant article on comic books is a good fit for *AntiqueWeek*, which chronicles not just collectibles, but also—when applicable—how collecting affects society. In two brief, clearly written paragraphs, I explained both the comic book and the controversy, along with an idea of what the article would contain.

■■■

Brett Weiss
817 - XXX - XXXX
brettw105@sbcglobal.net

Dear [Mr. or Ms. _____]:

In January longtime publisher Archie Comics will release *Life with Archie* #16, in which returning war hero Kevin Keller will marry his partner, an African-American male (meanwhile, Archie and Veronica are separated). *Life with Archie* is a magazine-sized comic book series taking place in the future, when Archie, Betty, Jughead, and the rest of the Riveredale gang are in their 20s.

How about a story on this release? It is sure to be a major news item and is already generating controversy. I can interview local comic book store owners/managers, discuss the history of gay characters in mainstream comic books, and talk a little about gay marriage in general. I'll also provide some history on Archie Comics and talk about how they are still popular with kids (and adults in many cases).

Query Subject: Geek Culture in Dallas/Fort Worth
Publication: Fort Worth Star-Telegram
Why this query worked: As evidenced by the popularity of *Doctor Who*, *The Big Bang Theory*, super-hero movies, and the like, geek culture is thriving. One day, shortly after looking over a comic book convention calendar for the Dallas/Fort Worth area, I discovered that PBS was going to air a new Wonder Woman documentary. It occurred to me in a flash that a feature on geek culture would be a good idea for the local newspaper. Fortunately, my editor at the Star-Telegram agreed. (Note: The word "budget" in the query is a newspaper term that refers to space availability, not available funds.)

∎∎

Brett Weiss
817 – XXX - XXXX
brettw105@sbcglobal.net

Dear [Mr. or Ms. _____]:

A lot of fun and exciting comic book events are scheduled in the area for April and May. I could do a comic book or geek culture feature spotlighting each event. On March 30, the Texas Lottery is promoting their Star Trek lottery tickets at the Irving Convention Center to try and break the Guinness record for most people in Star Trek costumes at one event, so it might be a good idea to run the comic book story around this time. William Shatner will appear.

If there's no budget around March 30, maybe early April?

April and May events include:

April 13: The next installment of the quarterly North Texas Comic Book Shows in Dallas, with vendors selling comics, action figures, and the like. In addition, Lone Star Comics has committed to spending up to $200,000 for comic book collections (if you have comics that you want to sell, you can bring them to the show and turn them into cash).

April 15: Wonder Woman documentary on PBS.

May 4: Free Comic Book Day, when participating comic book shops give away new comic books absolutely free.

May 17-19: Dallas Comic-Con, which will include such celebrities as William Shatner, Nathan Fillion, Richard Dean Anderson, and Ernie Hudson.

Interested in a comic book or geek culture story?

Query Subject: Halloween Movies for the Family
Publication: Fort Worth Star-Telegram
Why this query worked: Editors of daily newspapers like timely stories that are useful for the entire family. Plus, they like common themes with a little twist—in this case horror films for Halloween that aren't too scary.

∎∎∎

Brett Weiss
817 – XXX - XXXX
brettw105@sbcglobal.net

Dear [Mr. or Ms. _____]:

Horror movies typically bring to mind blood, guts, gore and gratuitous violence. For a family-friendly newspaper such as the *Star-Telegram*, it would be useful to publish a listing-with-commentary of Halloween-themed films that would be fun and appropriate for mom, dad, brother and sister.

My feature on "Halloween Fun—Family-Friendly Horror Films" (or something similar) would include such titles as *Mad Monster Party* (1969), *Ghostbusters* (1984), *The Addams Family* (1991), *Scooby Doo on Zombie Island* (1998) and *Wallace & Gromit: The Curse of the Were-Rabbit* (2005).

After a brief intro, in which I establish the family- and Halloween-centered premise, I will list 10 films and include fun, lively commentary for each. At the end, I will provide a listing of 10 more family-friendly horror films to consider.

My list will include a variety of films, both mainstream and relatively obscure—all readily available on DVD.

If you are interested in such a feature, please let me know.

Query Subject: Handheld Video Games for the Summer
Publication: Fort Worth Star-Telegram
Why this query worked: If I would have pitched an article on handheld gaming without the on-the-go-in-the-summer angle, this query might not have led to a paying job. Newspaper editors like publishing stories that have a timely, practical application. They like local angles as well, which is why I mentioned Six Flags.

●●

Brett Weiss
817 – XXX - XXXX
brettw105@sbcglobal.net

Dear [Mr. or Ms. _____]:

With people traveling during the summer, and with kids (and adults) wanting something to do while away from their home consoles, I believe this would be a great time for a roundup of handheld video games for the various mobile platforms, such as the iPhone, the Nintendo 3DS, and the PlayStation Vita.

There are many wonderful titles that casual and devoted gamers alike can play on the go, from a visit to the Louvre museum on the 3DS to some surprisingly sophisticated first-person shooters for the iPhone.

I'm talking about games that are currently available in stores or for digital download. In the lead, I'll emphasize how the games will give you something to do while in the car, at grandma's house, in line at Six Flags, in hotel rooms and the like.

Interested in a roundup of on-the-go games for the summer?

Query Subject: Heartwarming Movies
Publication: Fort Worth Star-Telegram
Why this query worked: When pitching a story for a particular newspaper or magazine, it's important to familiarize yourself with that publication. The previous year I had seen a summertime article (which I clipped out and saved) in the *Star-Telegram* on "Frozen Flicks," which listed films "to chill you out no matter how hot it gets outside." My article idea took the same basic approach, but flipped the seasons. I wasn't at all surprised the editor approved it.

■■■

Brett Weiss
817 – XXX - XXXX
brettw105@sbcglobal.net

Dear [Mr. or Ms. _____]:

With cold temperatures forecast for the foreseeable future, it's time for a story on movies that will warm the heart. My story will include a listing of 10 such films, each accompanied by a paragraph discussing the basic plot (and other particulars) and why the film is heartwarming.

The listing will be diverse and entertaining and will include such fare as *Rudy*, *Beauty and the Beast*, *The Miracle Worker* and *Mr. Smith Goes to Washington*.

Each film I'll include in the article will be accessible by a wide audience and readily available on DVD.

Please let me know if you are interested in such a feature.

Query Subject: Harry Houdini Collector Arthur Moses
Publication: AntiqueWeek
Why this query worked: Prior to pitching this article, I interviewed Houdini collector Arthur Moses, knowing he and his incredible collection would make for an interesting article and that I could probably find a home for it somewhere. This allowed for a colorful pitch, where I could describe the setting of his collection and even include quotes. Plus, Moses is not just an accumulator of stuff—he's a noted bibliographer, setting him apart from most collectors.

••

Brett Weiss
817 – XXX - XXXX
brettw105@sbcglobal.net

Dear [Mr. or Ms. _____]:

The author of the *Houdini Periodical Bibliography* (2006, H & R Magic Books) and *Houdini Speaks Out* (2007, Xlibris), Arthur Moses is the world's foremost Harry Houdini bibliographer, collecting, cataloging, and archiving more than 1500 Houdini-related books and more than 1400 Houdini-related periodicals. Moses also owns a vast array of Houdiniania, including vintage keys, handcuffs, magic kits, a straitjacket, movie posters, signed letters, personal effects, and much more.

A noted Houdini historian, Moses frequently speaks to various groups on the subject, and he entertains tour groups in his home (where I interviewed him). Famed magician David Copperfield once visited Moses to take a look at his collection, which is displayed beautifully in museum-like fashion (Moses owns a glass company and designs many of the displays himself).

A conscientious archivist, Moses maintains a good, long-term view of his prized possessions, and of his role in preserving Houdini's legend: "I'm just a caretaker," he says. "Someone owned this stuff before me, and someone's going to own it after me."

My article on Arthur Moses and his photogenic, carefully catalogued accumulation, which has taken a quarter of a century to acquire, will illuminate both the collector and his collection.

Query Subject: The Hunchback of Notre Dame
Publication: AntiqueWeek
Why this query worked: When brainstorming ideas, you should keep an eye out for key anniversaries related to the types of topics you want to write about (make Google your friend). With the Charles Laughton version of *The Hunchback of Notre Dame* approaching its 75th anniversary, I figured that it would be a good time for a story about the original novel and the various films it inspired. My editor at *AntiqueWeek* enthusiastically agreed.

■ ■

Brett Weiss
817 – XXX - XXXX
brettw105@sbcglobal.net

Dear [Mr. or Ms. _____]:

Written by Victor Hugo in 1831, *The Hunchback of Notre Dame* is one of the world's most enduring and endearing novels, telling the tale of the diminutive, put-upon Quasimodo and his love for Esmeralda. The book, which is still in print after all these years, has been adapted for television and film numerous times, including the masterful 1939 feature film starring Charles Laughton. The movie was released on Dec. 29, 1939, so it's approaching its 75th anniversary.

I think a story on *The Hunchback of Notre Dame* would make for a terrific cover feature for readers of all ages and tastes. I would cover the original novel, the adaptations, the collectibles, and more.

Query Subject: ICv2: Part-Time Freelancing Job
Website: ICv2.com
Why this query worked: When my brother-in-law sent me the link to an application for a freelancing gig for the geek culture news site, ICv2.com, I jumped at the chance, writing up a proposal touting my experience in the field. The query may seem a little cocky, but I wanted the editor to know that I was absolutely the right person for the job. Unlike article and book pitches, where you should only state your qualifications toward the end of the pitch, job applications require you to sell yourself right away.

■■■

Brett Weiss
817 – XXX - XXXX
brettw105@sbcglobal.net

Dear [Mr. or Ms. _____]:

At the risk of sounding immodest, I believe I have the ideal qualifications for writing for ICv2.

I'm a full-time freelancer, writing pop culture news articles and cover features for *AntiqueWeek*, comic book reviews for the *Comics Buyer's Guide*, and movie, business, and video game stories for a major metropolitan newspaper, the *Fort Worth Star-Telegram*.

I've also been published in *Fangoria*, *Filmfax*, *Back Issue*, *Alter Ego*, *Hogan's Alley*, *Game Informer*, *Video Game Collector*, *Video Game Trader*, *Classic Gamer Magazine*, *Toy Shop*, *Toy Car & Model*, *The Writer*, *Treasures*, *Robot* magazine, and various other publications.

I keep my finger on the pulse of geek culture and am an expert in such fields as film, television, comic books, video games, collectibles, antiques, and action figures. As a full-time writer, I specialize in the "quick turnaround," writing polished articles that typically need very little in the way of editing. When the *Star-Telegram* needs a story with a tight deadline, they often turn to me.

As the author of the *Classic Home Video Games* book series (McFarland Publishers), which catalogues video games from the golden age of gaming, I have concision down to a science. In addition, I was an editor and writer for the All Game Guide for several years, and I'm currently an archivist for mycomicshop.com.

I've attached published clips for your perusal. Please let me know if you have any questions or need more writing samples.

Query Subject: Indiana Jones and the Adventure of Archaeology: The Exhibition
Publication: AntiqueWeek
Why this query worked: While *AntiqueWeek* does publish pop culture features, the newspaper, as the name indicates, focuses on antiques, so the editor prefers ancient artifacts to modern collectibles, especially when it comes to cover stories. As such, when I proposed this article, I made sure to emphasize the archeological, educational items: note that the second paragraph is longer than the first.

■■

Brett Weiss
817 – XXX - XXXX
brettw105@sbcglobal.net

Dear [Mr. or Ms. _____]:

The Fort Worth Museum of Science and History is hosting "Indiana Jones and the Adventure of Archaeology: The Exhibition," which runs through August. It is an incredible exhibit, featuring props from all four films, including the Ark of the Covenant, Indy's hat and whip, Mutt Williams' Harley, and the Chacapoyan fertility idol.

"Indiana Jones and the Adventure of Archaeology" not only features a vast and exclusive collection of Indy props, models, concept art, and costumes, it also presents a wealth of historical and cultural facts and objects. The internationally renowned University of Pennsylvania Museum of Archaeology and Anthropology, otherwise known as the Penn Museum, is providing a remarkable array of archaeological artifacts and educational material. National Geographic, the exhibition's global presenting partner, also shares photos, videos and content from its impressive and historic archive.

I've gone to this exhibit, and it is truly impressive. Interested in a story about it for *AntiqueWeek*?

Query Subject: James Reasoner and Livia B. Washburn-Reasoner: Author Couple

Publication: The West Texan News

Why this query worked: This idea had a number of things going for it, so I figured rightly that it was an easy sale. Not only do the Reasoners write popular novels, and not only are they local, they lost everything through a house fire, but managed to rebuild and continue in their success. Since the Reasoners, though successful, aren't famous, I made sure to describe them in detail. I met the Reasoners through my brother-in-law and sister—it's important to exploit the people you know (and the people they know) to get good story ideas.

■■■

Brett Weiss
817 – XXX - XXXX
brettw105@sbcglobal.net

Dear [Mr. or Ms. _____]:

James Reasoner and Livia B. Washburn-Reasoner are successful novelists living in Azle. Both write mysteries, westerns, and other genre fiction.

James, a prolific author who often writes a million words in a single year, has written novels based on the *Walker, Texas Ranger* television series. He's written numerous other books, including the popular "Civil War Battle" series. His first book, *Texas Wind* (1980), was the first private eye novel based in Fort Worth.

In addition to writing, Livia proofreads her husband's novels and helps take care of her elderly parents. In short, Livia leads a busy life, but still manages to publish on a regular basis.

In 2008, the Reasoner's house burned to the ground, destroying their book collections, computers, manuscripts, and pretty much everything else they owned. In the years since, they've rebuilt their lives (as well as their house). Unlike many writers, the Reasoners, who grew up in Azle and went to high school there, support themselves solely through their writing.

I propose a feature on the Reasoners. The story will cover how they met, their house fire, their working relationship, their inspiration and motivations for writing, their commercial success (or lack thereof in some cases), the types of books they write, and much more. I'll sprinkle the article with plenty of quotes from James and Livia.

A full-time free-lancer, I've had articles published in the *Fort Worth Star-Telegram*, *The Writer*, *AntiqueWeek*, *Game Informer*, *Robot* magazine, and various other publications. I'm also the author of the *Classic Home Video Games* book series.

Please let me know if you are interested in a story on the Reasoners. I've attached published writing samples for your perusal.

Query Subject: James Reasoner: Prolific Author
Publication: The Writer
Why this query worked: As a writer, it's important for you to re-use what you write as often as possible in order to maximize both your time and your pay. I had already written about James Reasoner for *The West Texan News*, so when I was doing market research for *The Writer* and saw their "How I Write" column, I simply asked James a few more questions about his writing habits and repurposed some of what I had already written. Prior to writing this pitch, I read several installments of "How I Write" so I would know exactly what the editor of *The Writer* was looking for.

∎∎

Brett Weiss
817 – XXX - XXXX
brettw105@sbcglobal.net

Dear [Mr. or Ms. _____]:

Texas-based novelist and Spur Award nominee James Reasoner has written more than 200 books, both under his own name and under various pen names (including Dana Fuller Ross). He has agreed to be interviewed regarding his impressive career.

My interview with Mr. Reasoner will include: a 100-word bio; an examination of his daily writing routine; how he works with is writer wife; any advice he may have for aspiring writers; and how he rebounded from a recent fire that totally destroyed his house and all of his writing materials (including an unpublished manuscript he was working on).

If you are interested in an interview with James Reasoner, please let me know. I look forward to hearing from you.

I've attached my resume for your perusal.

Query Subject: Keep Watching the Skies! Book Review
Publication: Fangoria
Why this query worked: *Keep Watching the Skies!* is a landmark publication, bringing back into print a beloved two-volume work in one massive tome. As a freelancer, I frequently request review copies from a variety of publishers, and I knew an important work like this deserved to be written about. When pitching the idea to *Fangoria*, I made sure the editor was familiar with the book, and I made sure the editor knew I was a longtime *Fangoria* fan familiar with the magazine's book reviews column.

∎∎

Brett Weiss
817 – XXX - XXXX
brettw105@sbcglobal.net

Dear [Mr. or Ms. _____]:

I thoroughly enjoy Fango's "Nightmare Library" (I collect and read books voraciously) and am interested in submitting a review of Bill Warren's *Keep Watching the Skies!*, which, as you probably know, McFarland Publishers recently rereleased in a revised and expanded hardcover edition. (The official book launch is in March of 2010, but I've already got my review copy.)

I've been on the *Comics Buyer's Guide* review crew for almost a decade, having written hundreds of comic book reviews and various other features. I've also been published in *Back Issue*, *Alter Ego*, *Scary Monsters*, *Game Informer*, *Video Game Trader*, and a number of other publications.

A *Fangoria* fan for longer than I care to remember, I'm a "monster kid" (to borrow a term from Kerry Gammill) and a collector and reader of such magazines as *Filmfax*, *Castle of Frankenstein*, and *Famous Monsters*.

I've attached my resume and some published writing samples for your perusal. If you are interested in a review of *Keep Watching the Skies!*, please let me know.

Query Subject: Livia B. Washburn: Mystery Writer
Publication: Mystery Scene
Why this query worked: Once again, repurposing interviews and articles is a good idea. Since I had already written about Livia Washburn-Reasoner, who writes mystery novels as Livia B. Washburn, it only made sense to interview her again and tailor the new article toward mystery fans. I queried *Mystery Scene* and, at her request, called the editor shortly after a trip to Barnes & Noble, where I had perused the magazine racks, looking for markets to publish my work (something you should do on a regular basis).

■■

Brett Weiss
817 – XXX - XXXX
brettw105@sbcglobal.net

Dear [Mr. or Ms. _____]:

It was nice speaking to you on the phone. Thanks for listening to my pitch on an interview with Livia J. Washburn, author of the "Fresh Baked Mystery" and "Literary Tour Mystery" series.

Livia has a new trade paperback coming out in November of this year: *Gingerbread Bump-Off*, the sixth book in the "Fresh Baked" series.

Also in November, two of her titles will be released in mass market paperback for the first time: *The Pumpkin Muffin Murder*, which is the fifth "Fresh Baked" book; and *Killer on a Hot Tin Roof*, the third "Literary Tour" novel.

In addition to writing, Livia proofreads her husband James Reasoner's novels and helps take care of her elderly parents. A couple of years ago, her house burned to the ground. In short, Livia leads a busy life, but still manages to publish on a regular basis.

As we discussed, and if you are interested, I'll write the piece as a 900-word article with quotes. I'll begin the article with a couple of paragraphs about Livia's books, followed by information about the author herself: her motivation, style, work habits, etc.

I've had articles published in *The Writer*, *Filmfax*, *AntiqueWeek*, *Robot* magazine, *Toy Shop*, *Fangoria*, *Game Informer*, the *Fort Worth Star-Telegram*, and numerous other periodicals.

I've attached a couple of clips for your perusal.

Query Subject: Marilyn Monroe
Publication: AntiqueWeek
Why this query worked: Once again, keeping your ear to the ground for key anniversaries is a good idea for coming up with article pitches. Not only was it the 50th anniversary of the death of Marilyn Monroe, her legacy was being expanded even further by a new movie, a current television series, and the continued production of Marilyn Monroe merchandise.

■■■

Brett Weiss
817 – XXX - XXXX
brettw105@sbcglobal.net

Dear [Mr. or Ms. _____]:

Sunday is the 50th anniversary of the death of Marilyn Monroe. Numerous new and recent books on Monroe have been released, along with several new DVD sets. Michelle Williams recently received an Oscar nomination for her portrayal of Monroe in *My Week With Marylyn*. The hit TV show *Smash* revolves around the production of a Broadway musical based on Monroe's life.

In 2009, a commemorative Marilyn Monroe Barbie Doll was issued. Over the years, hundreds of Monroe collectibles have been released, including photos, magazines, postcards, wine bottles, calendars and too many other items to mention. In addition, her personal clothing, scripts, awards, furniture, kitchenware and glassware have been auctioned off over the years for millions of dollars.

In short, it's time for a collectibles-based Marilyn Monroe article. I could do an interior piece or a cover feature.

Interested?

Query Subject: Mike Begum: Competitive Gamer
Publication: Video Game Trader
Why this query worked: For a variety of reasons, including article ideas, writers should take full advantage of social media. On Facebook, one of my friends posted a link to a news feature about Mike Begum, a truly inspirational gamer. I found his story very compelling, as did the editor for *Video Game Trader*. In order for the editor to get the full effect of the obstacles Mr. Begum overcomes to play games, I included the YouTube link with my pitch.

■ ■

Brett Weiss
817 – XXX - XXXX
brettw105@sbcglobal.net

Dear [Mr. or Ms. _____]:

Mike Begum was born with arthrogryposis, a rare congenital disorder that causes severe joint contractures and muscle weakness. As such, his arms and legs, which are bent at odd angles, are largely useless for such ordinary endeavors as walking, driving, flexing, kicking, stretching, and picking up objects. As if that weren't enough of a cross to bear, he also has multiple scoliosis.

Despite these handicaps, Begum is a competitive video game player, traveling across the country to enter tournaments. He uses his mouth to push buttons on the controller, and he is great at fighting games. He recently wrote a book, and I interviewed him about his life and his devotion to and success in competitive gaming.

Are you interested in an article about Mr. Begum?

To help you decide, here's a short video about him:

https://www.youtube.com/watch?v=ECzN4fBkvTE

Query Subject: Non-Violent Video Games
Publication: Fort Worth Star-Telegram
Why this query worked: In the world we live in, tragedies occur, whether we write about them or not. When tragedy does strike, you might as well use it for a story idea, as I did here with the school shooting in Newtown, CT. I hate to be crass, and I was deeply saddened by the event, but story ideas are everywhere, especially in the darkest of places.

■ ■

Brett Weiss
817 – XXX - XXXX
brettw105@sbcglobal.net

Dear [Mr. or Ms. _____]:

The recent tragedy in Newtown, CT, in which a lone gunman fatally shot 20 children and six adults at Sandy Hook Elementary School, has the nation once again debating over gun ownership, mental health and violence in the media. The latter focus has primarily been over video games.

While it's true that many video games, especially today's photorealistic, first-person shooters (*Call of Duty*, *Halo* and the like), have death and destruction as key gameplay elements, studies are decidedly inconclusive regarding the negative effects playing violent video games may or may not have on the user. The debate is ongoing.

In addition, although video games are often considered synonymous with violence, there are plenty of non-violent games crowding store shelves. How about a roundup of 10 such games for current systems? I think concerned parents and educators will appreciate such a story.

My list will include such non-violent titles as *Lego Star Wars*, *NBA 2K13*, *Nintendo Land* and *LittleBigPlanet*.

Query Subject: North Texas Comic Book Shows
Publication: AntiqueWeek
Why this query worked: Instead of being a mere advertisement for a small, local comic-con, which the editor of AntiqueWeek, a national newspaper, probably would not have accepted, this story idea touched on several themes: small business success story, geek culture, and the star power of a guy like Lou "The Incredible Hulk" Ferrigno.

■■

Brett Weiss
817 – XXX - XXXX
brettw105@sbcglobal.net

Dear [Mr. or Ms. _____]:

Back in 2010, two comic book enthusiasts living in North Texas had a conversation about the lack of small, frequent conventions in the Dallas/Fort Worth area. The brainstorming session led to North Texas Comic Book Shows, a quarterly mini-con.

The first of the North Texas Comic Book Shows was held Oct. 21, 2011 at the Hilton Hotel, drawing just four dealers and 70 customers. The ensuing shows have grown exponentially—hundreds of guests are expected at the Jan. 5-6 Dallas show, which will feature Lou "The Incredible Hulk" Ferrigno is the guest star.

In addition to the Incredible Hulk, the show will feature a vendors room filled with retro action figures, classic comic books, vintage paperbacks, original art, super-hero model kits, old magazines, and other collectibles and curios.

North Texas Comic Book Shows is a small business success story, and having a guest like Lou Ferrigno only adds to the interest.

I could interview the CEO of North Texas Comic Book Shows and write up a story about the forthcoming show. Interested?

Why this query worked: Quickly and concisely, I summed up what the Oklahoma Alliance of Fans and its annual convention are all about.

■■

Brett Weiss
817 – XXX - XXXX
brettw105@sbcglobal.net

Dear [Mr. or Ms. _____]:

Short for the Oklahoma Alliance of Fans, OAF is a nostalgia club that was founded in 1967 for collectors of vintage movies, serials, wind-up toys, newspaper comics, dime novels, comic books, posters, science fiction material, original artwork, pulp magazines, advertising items, old-time radio shows, and many other forms of nostalgia.

OAF, which reformed in 2007 for its 40th anniversary, now holds a convention each year, in which dealers set up tables to sell these types of items. Numerous original members attend and always have great stories to tell about the early days of fandom.

This year's event is Nov. 11 and 12 at the Biltmore Hotel in Oklahoma City. In addition to dealers selling thousands of vintage items, the convention will host an auction, film screenings, and book signings.

Are you interested in a news article about this convention?

Query Subject: Penguins in Pop Culture
Publication: Fort Worth Star-Telegram
Why this query worked: When I read the *Fort Worth Star-Telegram*, I clip and save articles that I might find useful. One story I kept was about monkeys in popular culture, which coincided with a new *Planet of the Apes* film. When *Penguins 3D* was announced, I fired off this query on penguins in pop culture, which the editor quickly accepted. In fact, one thing I do on a regular basis is scan listings of forthcoming movies, books, CDs, video games, and other media, finding article ideas where I can.

■■

Brett Weiss
817 – XXX - XXXX
brettw105@sbcglobal.net

Dear [Mr. or Ms. _____]:

With *Penguins 3D* releasing May 24, I thought it would be fun to write a penguins in pop culture story. I would include penguins in literature, film, video games, cartoons, music, sports teams and more.

The story will begin with a general mention of how penguins are found in various forms of pop culture. Then I will discuss real penguins for one paragraph. Then, the main body of the story will feature such penguins in pop culture as Tennessee Tuxedo, The Penguin super-villain, Bloom County, the Pittsburgh Penguins hockey team, the video game *Pengo*, March of the Penguins, Farce of the Penguins and more.

Interested in a story on penguins in pop culture?

Query Subject: Prince in Comic Books
Publication: Back Issue
Why this query worked: When the editor for *Back Issue* magazine sent out a memo to his stable of freelancers saying he wanted pitches for articles on comic book "royalty" (kings, queens, and the like), I threw a curveball, suggesting a feature on the rock star Prince, who had appeared in a couple of DC comics. Editors like original ideas, and this one certainly qualified.

■■

Brett Weiss
817 – XXX - XXXX
brettw105@sbcglobal.net

Dear [Mr. or Ms. _____]:

Who is the most famous prince in the history of comic books? Prince Valiant? Prince Namor? Diana Prince? Wrong, wrong, and wrong. With apologies to Hal Foster, Bill Everett, and Charles Moulton (respective creators of the aforementioned princes who wouldn't be king), the most well -known comic book prince is, well, Prince, the eccentric rock star who made his splash during the 1980s with such flashy, funky pop songs as "Little Red Corvette," "When Doves Cry," and "Delirious," and who continues to thrill pop music fans today.

You may be wondering: What in the wild, wild world of sports does Prince have to do with comic books? In 1991, during a boom of sorts for music-based comic books (thanks in part to Revolutionary, the publisher of such titles as the *Led Zeppelin Experience*), DC Comics, under its Piranha Music label, released *Prince: Alter Ego*, a one-shot written by Dwayne McDuffie (*Justice League Unlimited*), penciled by Denys Cowan (*The Question*), and inked by Kent Williams (*Havok & Wolverine: Meltdown*). A follow-up issue was released as well.

I could write a compelling article on the Prince comics published by DC, especially given the fact that I was a comic book retailer when those issues came out. I could put them in their proper context (as you probably remember, there were a lot of rock comics being published at the time), encapsulate the storylines, comment on the art, and touch a little bit on Prince himself and on the imprint that DC used in publishing the comics.

Query Subject: Road Movies
Publication: Fort Worth Star-Telegram
Why this query worked: While scanning an online list of forthcoming feature films, I saw a listing for *Road to Paloma*, the title of which reminded me of the old Bob Hope/Bing Crosby road pictures. It also occurred to me that the road movie is a viable genre, and that it would make for a good summer feature for the *Star-Telegram*. Luckily, the editor, who probably appreciated the versatile nature of the genre, agreed.

■■

Brett Weiss
817 – XXX - XXXX
brettw105@sbcglobal.net

Dear [Mr. or Ms. _____]:

Summer is a great time to gas up the "family truckster" and hit the road, whether you want to travel cross country or simply dash up to WinStar Casino for a little gambling or down to Austin for some primo live music.

It's also a great time to watch a road movie. How about a roundup of road films, set to coincide with the release of the new road movie, *Road to Paloma*, which releases July 11?

My lead will discuss summer being a good time to take a road trip, but that you can also enjoy a road trip from the comfort of your couch. My lead will also discuss the release of *Road to Paloma*, which stars Jason Momoa, Robert Homer Mollohan and Lisa Bonet.

My roundup will include 10 road movies, including such films as *National Lampoon's Vacation*, *Smokey and the Bandit*, *Easy Rider*, *Little Miss Sunshine* and *Road to Singapore*.

It will be a nice mix of classic and newer films.

Interested in a roundup of road movies?

Query Subject: Rock Gods Gone Solo
Publication: Fort Worth Star-Telegram
Why this query worked: I had done a number of movie roundups for the *Star-Telegram* by this point, so I figured it was time for a music round-up. When I read about Paul McCartney recording a new solo album, I came up with the idea of an article about rock gods who had gone solo. The idea was fairly original (if not entirely unique), and it turned out to be one of the most popular articles I've ever written for the *Star-Telegram* (assuming Facebook "likes" and comments are any indication).

■■■

Brett Weiss
817 – XXX - XXXX
brettw105@sbcglobal.net

Dear [Mr. or Ms. _____]:

I have what I think is a fun and interesting idea for a story. Paul McCartney's new solo album, entitled *New*, is coming out Oct. 15. Backed by a Beatles-esque single (also called "New"), which began receiving airplay late last month, the CD is highly anticipated by McCartney fans and Beatlemaniacs alike.

With this in mind, how about a roundup of solo albums by rock-and-roll legends who are famous for fronting a popular band?

Rock icons like Ozzy, David Lee Roth, Mick Jagger, Paul Stanley, Roger Daltrey, Stevie Nicks and Robert Plant have each put out memorable solo records. I would spot light 10 such releases and include commentary on each artist and each record. The format would be similar to my movie roundups.

Interested in a story about solo albums by famous rock and roll front men?

Query Subject: Slot Car Racing
Publication: Toy Cars & Models
Why this query worked: Instead of proposing a pitch for a simple history of slot car racing, I made it a more personal story, thanks to the fact that I happen to have a friend who is heavily into the hobby. Finding a suitable publication was easy since another friend of mine happens to write for it. Writers should use everything at their disposal to get published as often as possible, including friends.

▪▪

Brett Weiss
817 – XXX - XXXX
brettw105@sbcglobal.net

Dear [Mr. or Ms. _____]:

I know a couple of gentlemen who are avid slot car enthusiasts, racing most weekends into the wee hours of the morning. They frequently purchase new tracks and cars, set up lots of different layouts, and have themed races (dinosaurs, robots, and the like) with accompanying scenery.

The slot car racers in question are brothers and were into the hobby back in the late sixties and throughout seventies as well. My article will discuss their entry into the hobby, their continued interest in slot car racing, and the specific rules they use for races they had as kids and today.

I'm on the *Comics Buyer's Guide* review crew and got your contact information from Rick Kelsey, a friend of mine who contributes frequently to your fine publication.

Are you interested in an article on slot car racing for *Toy Cars & Models*?

Query Subject: Spidey Super Stories
Publication: Filmfax
Why this query worked: Just in case the editor for *Filmfax* wasn't familiar with "Spidey Super Stories," I went into great detail regarding the skit. In fact, it's usually a good idea to provide plenty of detail in your queries. Not only does it tell the editor what the article will be about, it shows that you are well-versed on the subject. I made sure to mention the fact that a then-unknown Morgan Freeman was in the show, an aspect that lent star power to the pitch.

■■

Brett Weiss
817 – XXX - XXXX
brettw105@sbcglobal.net

Dear [Mr. or Ms. _____]:

How about an article on "Spidey Super Stories," the truly bizarre recurring skit on *The Electric Company*? Many *Filmfax* readers grew up watching *The Electric Company*, and some of us watched it solely for *Super Spidey Stories*.

Introduced by a memorable theme song (*Spider-Man, where are you coming from? Spider-Man, nobody knows who you are!*), each installment of "Spidey Super Stories" lasted approximately three to six minutes, which was just enough time to play out a simple story involving a goofy villain (always an original creation, never a bad guy from the comics), a curiously (and often crazily) devised crime, and a resultant save from Marvel Comics' friendly neighborhood flagship character.

The great Morgan Freeman appeared in "Super Spidey Stories" as a variety of colorful characters. In "A Night at the Movies," Freeman does his best Bela Lugosi impersonation as Dracula (insert Blacula reference/joke here), sneaking up behind a moviegoer, trying to bite her on the neck. Other roles Freeman played in *Spidey Super Stories* include a police officer in "Dr. Fly," a mad scientist in "The Beastly Banana," and Easy Reader in "The Bookworm."

In addition to production history, comical plot synopses, and the like, my article will include interviews with Jean Thomas (Roy Thomas' wife) and Jim Salicrup, both of whom worked on the comic book version of the show.

Please let me know if you are interested in an article on "Super Spidey Stories," one of the strangest shows in the annals of super-hero history. I do have art for the article.

Query Subject: Stephen King
Publication: Filmfax
Why this query worked: Much has been written about Stephen King over the years, but few people know anything about when or where his first story was published. So I did a little investigative work, conducted some interviews, and wrote the article, confident that such an unusual piece would find a home. Editors love an unusual slant on a popular topic.

■■

Brett Weiss
817 – XXX - XXXX
brettw105@sbcglobal.net

Dear [Mr. or Ms. _____]:

For years a great deal of mystery has surrounded the origins of Stephen King's first published story. In fact, King himself, in his nonfiction book, *On Writing*, misremembered the facts of when and where his first story was published.

To clear up this mystery, I contacted Michael Garrett, who serialized "I Was a Teenage Grave Robber" in 1965 in four issues of his fanzine, *Comics Review*. Famed comic book writer Marv Wolfman then republished the story in his fanzine, *Stories of Suspense*, renaming the tale "In a Half-World of Terror."

With this (and other) information in hand, I wrote an article on King's first published story, fleshing out said article by interviewing two Stephen King collectors, including David Williams, who owns an online King specialty store called Betts Books.

I'm a full-time freelancer, writing for the *Fort Worth Star-Telegram* and numerous other publications. I'm also the author of the *Classic Home Video Games* book series (McFarland Publishers).

Query Subject: Superman vs. Muhammad Ali
Publication: Back Issue
Why this query worked: When the editor for *Back Issue* magazine sent out a memo wanting pitches for articles about the legendary tabloid comic book, *Superman vs. Muhammad Ali*, I was excited because I had a story to tell about my cousin giving me the issue when I was a kid. I wasn't privy to the other writers' pitches, of course, but I made it a point to write a colorful, compelling, and contextual query that he couldn't refuse.

■■■

Brett Weiss
817 – XXX - XXXX
brettw105@sbcglobal.net

Dear [Mr. or Ms. _____]:

I know you'll get a lot of requests for this topic, but I'd like to throw my hat in the ring for SUPERMAN VS. MUHAMMAD ALI. Not only do I collect tabloid-sized comic books, but that's a very special issue to me.

Obviously, I loved comics as a kid. I couldn't always afford what I wanted to buy, but my older cousin had a huge collection, and I would spend hours in his room, reading *Savage Sword, Fantastic Four, Vampirella, Iron Man, Amazing Spider-Man*, etc. (I already had plenty of DCs, and another cousin had Dells and Harveys).

Outside of maybe Superman and Muhammad Ali, I thought my cousin was the coolest person on the planet—I worshipped the ground he walked on. One day while he was at my house, a few months after the issue came out, he handed me his copy of SUPERMAN VS. MUHAMMAD ALI and said I could have it.

Needless to say, I was floored. Not only had Zeus come down from Mount Olympus to give me, a mere mortal, a priceless treasure, I had never even seen such a gigantic comic book. I loved the story and was absolutely blown away by the art. Neal Adams is greatness, of course, but seeing his masterful work at that size was STUNNING. And I LOVED the celebrities featured on the cover and the accompanying code on the inside. Moreover, seeing Superman battered to a pulp was at once frightening and intriguing—I'll never forget those bruises on his face!

My article will have some anecdotal information, but, more importantly, it will encapsulate the story, put the issue in the context of the times (when the sweet science in general and Ali in particular were such an important part of Americana—not at all like boxing today, which is a shell of its former self), and reference such previous titanic battles as FRANKENSTEIN MEETS THE WOLFMAN, KING KONG VS. GODILLA, SUPERMAN VS. THE AMAZING SPIDER-MAN, and the like.

And it shouldn't be too difficult to get some quotes from Denny O'Neil and/or Neal Adams.

Query Subject: The Texas Rangers
Publication: AntiqueWeek
Why this query worked: Before I submitted this pitch, I actually visited the Texas Rangers Museum, which is about an hour-and-a-half from my house. Since this was a place some friends and I had been wanting to visit anyway, it was a great excuse to take a fun road trip that I could write off as a business expense. Plus, I got in for free. As a writer, you should write off vehicle mileage, restaurant receipts, and like, as long as they pertain to your work. Regarding the acceptance of the pitch by the editor, I'm sure at least three things made an impression on her: I went to the museum, the museum was turning 50, and I promised to get quotes from the media relations person.

••

Brett Weiss
817 – XXX - XXXX
brettw105@sbcglobal.net

Dear [Mr. or Ms. _____]:

I recently visited the Texas Rangers Museum in Waco. It was really cool. The Texas Rangers law enforcement organization was unofficially organized by Stephen F. Austin in 1823 and was later made official. It began as a small militia force protecting settlers in the then Mexican province of Tejas.

The Texas Rangers still exist today, and the museum is filled with many interesting artifacts, including vintage guns and items confiscated by the Rangers over the years. There's even a pop culture section with exhibits on *Walker, Texas Ranger* and *The Lone Ranger*.

The media relations person with the museum has agreed to an interview--the Texas Rangers Museum turned 50 this year.

I believe the Texas Rangers would make for a fascinating cover feature.

Query Subject: Thundarr the Barbarian
Publication: Back Issue
Why this query worked: When *Back Issue* magazine announced a
Steve Gerber tribute issue, I was genuinely excited at the prospect of
writing about *Thundarr the Barbarian*, one of my favorite cartoons
as a kid. I think my enthusiasm shows in the pitch.

■■■

Brett Weiss
817 – XXX - XXXX
brettw105@sbcglobal.net

Dear [Mr. or Ms. _____]:

Publishing a Steve Gerber tribute is a wonderful idea. I was thrilled
to see *Thundarr the Barbarian* as an available assignment. For years,
I have been wanting to write an article about that show.

I watched *Thundarr* religiously when it first aired and was struck by
how unusual it was for Saturday morning fare. I was 14 at the time
and already a huge fan of *Savage Sword of Conan*, so it was very
cool to see something on TV that was Conan-esque. In short, I loved
the series (and still enjoy it today).

My *Thundarr* article will cover the basic plot of the series (including
analysis of certain specific episodes), the various creators involved
(Gerber, Kirby, Toth, Alcala, story board artists John Dorman and
Hank Tunker, and others), how the show pre-dated *He-Man*, how it
compared to other cartoons at the time (including the *Super
Friends*), and how it holds up today.

I collect old magazines about comics, so I will use a quotes from
magazines that were on newsstands when the series originally aired,
such as *The Comic Times* and *Comics Feature*. I will also endeavor
to get some new quotes, maybe even from someone like *Thundarr*
writer Roy Thomas, to see what he thought/thinks of the show.

If you give me this assignment, I know you will be pleased with the result. My article will be fun, informative, thoroughly researched, and professional in nature.

Query Subject: To Kill a Mockingbird
Publication: AntiqueWeek
Why this query worked: Once again, by staying on top of anniversaries for various forms of media (an iconic book in this case), I was able to write a timely, convincing pitch about an interesting topic. *To Kill a Mockingbird* is an indispensable story about racial prejudice, and the 50th anniversary of the film deserved cover-feature treatment.

■■

Brett Weiss
817 – XXX - XXXX
brettw105@sbcglobal.net

Dear [Mr. or Ms. _____]:

The film version of *To Kill a Mockingbird* turns 50 this Christmas. I could write a cover story on the novel and the film and include quotes from Nathan Carter, Director of Sites & Operations for the Monroe County Heritage Museum in Alabama, which includes an elaborate Harper Lee/To Kill a Mockingbird exhibit.

To Kill a Mockingbird is one of the most influential and studied novels in the history of publishing, and the film is highly acclaimed as well, ranked 25th best on AFI's 100 Years...100 Movies (10th Anniversary Edition).

If you are interested in a feature on *To Kill a Mockingbird*, please let me know. I'll cover Harper Lee's life, the publishing history of the book, the differences between the book and the film and more.

Query Subject: Valentine's Day Films Men and Women Can Enjoy
Publication: Fort Worth Star-Telegram
Why this query worked: If I had pitched an article about romantic movies for Valentine's Day, but didn't include an unusual angle or a twist, this query likely would have been rejected. However, by suggesting romantic films that even men will enjoy, the query made the cut. I also think my suggestion of eating out on the 13th (to avoid crowds) and watching films on the actual holiday was a good selling point of the pitch.

■■■

Brett Weiss
817 – XXX - XXXX
brettw105@sbcglobal.net

Dear [Mr. or Ms. _____]:

Valentine's Day will be here before you know it, and it's time to start thinking about how to celebrate the holiday. Restaurants are notoriously busy on the 14th, so I recommend eating out on the 13th and taking in a movie at home Valentine's Day night.

How about a feature on romantic films that both men and women can enjoy? I will list 10 films from a variety of genres representing a number of eras, from the 1930s to modern times. In addition to a brief plot synopsis for each film, I will mention why men can enjoy the film as well as women. Each film will be readily available on DVD.

I strongly believe that this story will make Valentine's Day more fun, more romantic and less stressful for *Star-Telegram* readers.

Please let me know if you are interested such a story.

Query Subject: Video Game Board Games
Publication: Video Game Trader
Why this query worked: The editor of *Video Game Trader* likes pitches about video game-related articles on unconventional subjects (he wouldn't want a standard review of a widely published, newly released game by a big company, for example), and this one certainly qualifies. Video game board games are niche market items that appeal to the type of hardcore gamers/collectors *Video Game Trader* caters to.

■■■

Brett Weiss
817 – XXX - XXXX
brettw105@sbcglobal.net

Dear [Mr. or Ms. _____]:

Board games are a popular pastime, as are video games. Why not combine the two?

During the Golden Age of Video Games, publishers were doing just that. Such companies as Milton Bradley and Parker Brothers produced such video game-based board games as *Centipede*, *Defender*, *Donkey Kong*, *Frogger*, *Jungle Hunt*, *Pac-Man*, *Popeye*, *Q*bert*, *Turbo*, and *Zaxxon*.

Like standard board games, these curious creations included such trappings as dice, marbles, spinners, tokens, cards, and, of course, fold-out boards. Obviously, rules varied from game to game, with some adhering very nicely to the spirit of the arcade original.

In the late 1980s and on through the '90s, such popular video games as *Street Fighter II*, *Teenage Mutant Ninja Turtles*, *Double Dragon*, *Sonic the Hedgehog*, *The Legend of Zelda*, and *Super Mario Bros.* were translated into board games.

And, during the last decade, video game-based board games have reached a new peak in popularity, with publishers producing such titles as *BioShock Infinite: The Siege of Columbia* and *World of Warcraft: The Boardgame*.

How about an article on video game-based board games? I've got collectors to interview and all the information I'll need in coming up with a fun, colorful story on the subject.

Query Subject: Video Game Gift Guide
Publication: Fort Worth Star-Telegram
Why this query worked: Instead of pitching a video game gift guide that recommended all the popular titles, I went for something a little different: peripheral items that appeal to gamers. Not only are these items likely to surprise the recipients with something they don't already own, they make for colorful write-ups. Again, it's a common theme—holiday gift guide—but with a twist.

■■■

Brett Weiss
817 – XXX - XXXX
brettw105@sbcglobal.net

Dear [Mr. or Ms. _____]:

Most everyone has a video game player in their life—a son, a brother, a niece, a nephew, a friend, a spouse, a neighbor. However, gamers are hard to buy for. Gift certificates are boring, and if you get them an actual videogame, you run the risk of duplicating something they already have, or getting them a game they won't like.

So, I propose a video game swag gift guide, spotlighting videogame-related items the gamers in question probably don't already own, but would love to. There are numerous nifty items of this type, including graphic novels, books about videogames, collector's sets, special controllers, clothing and more.

My video game holiday gift guide will feature 10-20 special items that would make for nifty Christmas gifts.

Please let me know if you are interested in such a story.

Query Subject: Vincent Van Gogh
Publication: AntiqueWeek
Why this query worked: For a query to convince an editor, it has to be well-written. It doesn't have to be the "great American essay," but it does need to be clear, concise, coherent, and free of grammatical errors, all the while including plenty of detail and color. I believe my Van Gogh pitch qualifies.

■ ■

Brett Weiss
817 – XXX - XXXX
brettw105@sbcglobal.net

Dear [Mr. or Ms. _____]:

I've been a fan of impressionism (and post-impressionism) for more than 20 years, and Van Gogh is my all-time favorite painter. I was particularly moved by *Dear Theo: The Autobiography of Vincent Van Gogh*, which tells his story via intimate letters to his brother.

There's nothing quite like seeing an original Van Gogh in person—the color, the thick brush strokes, the obvious passion he put into each painting. The image of a Van Gogh original will emblazon itself on your memory for years (at least it has for me on more than one occasion).

My article will cover the history of Van Gogh, along with the incredible sums paid for his paintings. To avoid alienating the average collector, I'll also cover more affordable Van Gogh items, such as books, prints, posters, belt buckles, mouse pads, coffee mugs, and the like.

My Van Gogh article will appeal to casual collectors and art fans, as well as dedicated disciples of the Dutch artist.

Interested?

Query Subject: Waylon Jennings
Publication: AntiqueWeek
Why this query worked: By reading newspapers and news websites, you can stay on top of current events, of course, but you can also get some great article ideas. When I saw in the *Fort Worth Star-Telegram* that Jessie Colter was selling off her diseased husband's stuff, I immediately cranked out this pitch, which points out the importance of Jennings himself along with the coolness of the items offered.

■■■

Brett Weiss
817 – XXX - XXXX
brettw105@sbcglobal.net

Dear [Mr. or Ms. _____]:

The late, great Waylon Jennings is an American treasure. Not only did he sing the iconic theme to *The Dukes of Hazzard*, he's known for such crossover classics as "Mamas Don't Let Your Babies Grow Up to Be Cowboys," "Good Hearted Woman," and "Luckenbach, Texas." Further, he teamed with fellow legends Johnny Cash, Kris Kristofferson, and Willie Nelson on many memorable occasions.

On Oct. 5 New York City-based auction house Guernsey's will hold an auction at the Musical Instrument Museum in Phoenix, featuring more than 2,000 personal items from his estate, including gold records, signed documents, a rare 1958 motorcycle once owned by Buddy Holly, and locks of Willie Nelson's braided hair, which Nelson cut off to show support for Jennings' sobriety. Jennings' widow, Jesse Colter, authorized the sale.

Are you interested in a Waylon Jennings auction report?

Query Subject: World's Largest Comic Book Collection
Publication: AntiqueWeek
Why this query worked: World records in and of themselves are fascinating—why would a human being go to such lengths to have the longest beard, create the largest ball of twine, or walk farther across the planet than anyone else? For a newspaper like *AntiqueWeek*, which focuses much of its square footage on collecting, a report on the world's largest comic book collection was an excellent fit. I heard about the record through Facebook, which on any given day harbors a wealth of article ideas.

■■■

Brett Weiss
817 – XXX - XXXX
brettw105@sbcglobal.net

Dear [Mr. or Ms. _____]:

Bob Bretall, a 52-year-old man living in Mission Viejo, California, has more comic books than you. Probably a whole lot more. At last official count, Bretall's collection consisted of 94,268 unique individual issues.

That final tally was conducted on May 1 at Bretall's home by the folks at Guinness, ensuring his spot in the 2014 edition of the *Guinness World Records* (formerly the *Guinness Book of World Records*). He's featured on page 172, though he says he's lost 88 pounds since that photo was taken. He also says he's added more than 1,000 comics to his collection.

Bretall says he doesn't collect for investment, but because of the "great stories and characters." He has plenty of other interesting things to say as well.

Interested in a cover feature on Bob Bretall and the world's largest comic book collection?

Breakthrough

A lifelong reader, I love perusing the printed page—books, magazines, newspapers, comic-books—you name it. And I've always wanted to be a writer. However, I never seriously pursued this longing until 1993, when I sold my business (a pair of comic-book stores) and suddenly found myself with plenty of time to write.

My first goal was to learn the craft and get published, which I did in 1997—a whopping $10 sale to an online fiction magazine. I continued cranking out short stories, but only found limited success, netting a sale here and there in an assortment of long-forgotten small-press magazines. Undeterred, I kept plugging away: read-write-repeat.

How I Broke Through

In 1998, my brother-in-law emailed me a classified ad for the All Game Guide (www.allgame.com), a database cataloging, describing, and reviewing every video-game ever released. As an avid video-game collector, I jumped on this opportunity and quickly got the job.

My part-time All Game Guide gig transformed into a highly profitable (relatively speaking) writing/editing position, inspiring me to seek additional non-fiction venues, including the *Comics Buyer's Guide*, where I became a member of the long-running magazine's Review Crew.

Unfortunately, after the terrorist attacks of 9/11 and the resultant economic downturn, the All Game Guide released its off-site writers, leaving me frustrated and heartbroken. I discussed this with a friend, who happened to own a garage door company. He offered me a job as a dispatcher, which let me work at home and gave me plenty of time to write between phone calls.

In 2006, I attended Comic-Con International in San Diego, where I talked with and gave a business card to an editor working for McFarland Publishers. Much to my surprise, she emailed me a few days later, asking if I had any interesting book ideas.

Thus, my *Classic Home Video Games* book series was born (the third volume was released in the fall of 2011), a project that looks good on my resume and has helped me get countless freelance assignments, including steady work for *AntiqueWeek*, *Filmfax*, the *Fort Worth Star-Telegram*, and various other publications.

What I learned

For most writers, especially those of us who didn't exactly excel in school, writing clean copy doesn't come naturally, no matter how much you have read or how much you have dreamed of one day becoming a writer. You have to work at it every day, whether you are getting published on a regular basis or not.

Without writing all those bad short stories, I may not have been able to work my way up to editor with the All Game Guide. Without writing hundreds of reviews for the All Game Guide and the *Comics Buyer's Guide*, my writing probably would've lacked the polish to justify a book contract. In short, I learned that real, working writers write constantly and feel compelled to do so.

Advice

Begin each day by waking up a couple of hours before everyone else, fixing yourself a strong caffeinated drink, and getting in some time at the computer or word processor while you are fresh and the house is quiet—you'll soon find yourself looking forward to this morning ritual.

Act like a professional, even if you haven't had a single word published. Call yourself a writer, establish a fully outfitted office area in your home, and keep business cards in your purse or wallet. Carry a notebook wherever you go, jotting down anything interesting you may hear someone say or any idea that might pop into your head.

Keep an organized filing system containing such things as publisher contact information, query letters, story ideas, and rejection and acceptance notices. Never throw away anything you have written, no matter how bad. That terrible piece you wrote years ago could provide the skeleton of an idea for a terrific screenplay or novel.

Prior to submitting an article or a story (or even a query), read at least a couple of issues of that publication to get a feel for what they publish (free sample copies or PDF files are often available online). No matter how sparkling your prose or how clever your turn of phrase, ill-fitting, inappropriate material will be rejected every time.

*This article originally appeared in the Nov. 2010 issue of *You & Me Medical Magazine*.

Anatomy of a Near Nervous Breakdown

Most every morning I get up before sunrise, pour myself a cup of steaming Earl Grey, and sit down at my computer to write—it's how I make a living. I've been following this routine for years, and I love it.

A few months ago, I tried to begin my work workday one morning, but I flat-out couldn't do it. As I stared at the blank "page" on the computer monitor, hot tea, breakfast bar, and research materials by my side, I felt anxious, unable to concentrate. I couldn't sit still, and my brain was buzzing with nervous energy. I had to get up and do something—anything. Anything other than write, that is.

To calm myself and get a clear, fresh focus on my work, I took a walk around the neighborhood. Maybe after a brisk walk and a hot shower, I reasoned, my mind would be calm enough for me to side down and string some coherent sentences together.

The walk was indeed refreshing, as was the shower, but my attempt at writing was futile. I simply sat before my now useless computer, sipping reheated tea and trying to focus on the subject matter at hand. The article in question was a proposed 6,000-word feature on the comic book hero, The Flash. This is longer than most articles I write, so I was a little anxious about it to begin with, but I like the character, so I was looking forward to it as well.

As I sat there, piles of comic books all around me, I couldn't decide how to start the article. I tried rereading a few of the comics for inspiration, but I couldn't focus long enough to follow even a simple comic book story. The longer I sat there, the more anxious I got, the more nervous I got. For the first time in my life, I felt a panic attack coming on.

I got up from my desk, my heart pounding as though I had just run a 50-yard-dash. I went to the game room to watch a goofy sitcom, hoping it would somehow calm me. I sat there on the couch, anxious, unable to enjoy the program. As I quickly got up to turn off the television set, I felt lightheaded. I had gotten up too fast. I paused and put my arms out to steady myself, but the dizziness increased, and suddenly everything went white.

I had fainted dead away.

The next thing I knew I was lying on the floor, my limbs scattered about randomly like jackstraws. As I opened my eyes, I could blurrily see that my glasses were lying on the carpet a few feet away. I felt sore, as though I had been punched in the face by Mike Tyson. A pile of DVDs that had been stacked on the entertainment center was spread across the floor.

After doing a little rudimentary investigative work, I reasoned out that I had banged my face against the entertainment center as I fell. I had only been out for a few seconds, but waking up on the floor, disheveled and disoriented, was truly a surreal—and highly disturbing—sensation.

Over the next couple of weeks, every time I sat down to write it was virtually impossible to get anything done. I managed to bang out a couple of reviews, but that was about it. I was too nervous, too antsy, too anxious, too flustered, too wormy, too scattered-brained, and too jittery. I was simply feeling too crazy to concentrate. I got plenty of housework done (what with the nervous energy and all), but very little writing.

I've always prided myself on having an evenly keeled disposition, a rational mind, and a strong work ethic, so my status as a panic attack victim made me feel like a failure and even a flake. Not only was I having trouble working, it was getting difficult to do such commonplace things as drive and read, both of which require sitting still and concentrating.

A couple of weeks or so later, I truly hit rock bottom (as though fainting wasn't rock bottom). After another in a series of largely unsuccessful work mornings, I went downstairs for lunch, fixed myself a sandwich, sat down to eat, and simply stared at my plate. I suddenly wasn't hungry. My heart started pounding against my shirt, panic began to set in, and I found myself gasping to breathe. I walked outside for some fresh air, but I literally felt like a fish out of water.

My wife took me to the local "doc in the box" (I didn't have a primary care physician at the time), and they subjected me to a series of tests, including an EKG. Everything was fine, at least according to their instruments, so the doctor recommended further testing via a heart specialist and a neurologist. I hated the thought of more doctor appointments, but I was eager to find out what was wrong and get it fixed. I simply had to get back to work (I couldn't afford not to).

After a series of appointments, treatments, and tests, including an uncomfortable 48-hour stint wearing a heart monitor, no cause was found for my condition. As I was about to leave what would turn out to be the last of my appointments, the doctor casually asked if I had been sleeping well. I told him that I had insomnia on a fairly regular basis. He suggested I cut down on caffeine.

Instead of simply cutting down on caffeine, I immediately eliminated it from my diet altogether. I gave up soda, chocolate, and even my beloved Earl Grey tea. Miraculously, all my symptoms—the nervousness, the anxiety, the muddled thinking, the heart palpitations, the shortness of breath, and the insomnia—disappeared almost overnight.

Apparently, after years of imbibing the stuff, my body had suddenly developed a severe intolerance to caffeine. I had always heard that caffeine was a drug, and there are certainly plenty of people addicted to coffee (and, to a lesser extent, tea), but I had never given the hazards of caffeine addiction much thought. I just knew that tea was good for you (certain studies show that it reduces the risk of getting cancer), and that I had grown dependant on its energizing effects for my writing career.

It seems dumb in hindsight, but it never occurred to me that my beloved Earl Grey could be the cause of my problems. During my illness my symptoms had been less severe on the weekends, but I had just assumed it was because there were no work-related pressures. It was actually because I hadn't been drinking two and three cups of tea on those mornings.

A couple of days after I gave up caffeine cold turkey, I was up bright and early, working away at my computer, the words flowing freely and quickly. I was feeling a little groggy, but I felt calm, cool, and collected. I'll take groggy over crazy any day.

These days I sip a little tea or diet soda every morning as I work, but I'm careful not to overindulge. If there's a moral to this story it's that it is indeed possible to have too much of a good thing.

How to Get Published

In the introduction to this book, I wrote that "most any reasonably intelligent person with a strong work ethic and a love for reading and writing can get published." If my career is any indication, this aphorism is as true as the equation $2 + 2 = 4$. However, all four criteria must be met: intelligence, hard work, and voracious reading and writing.

"Intelligence" may be a subjective term, and it's clear that some people were born smarter than others, but there are ways for even those of us with average I.Q.s to increase our intelligence. The two primary ways to do this are through reading and experiencing the world around you.

Instead of reading only what you like, read subject matter that goes against your strongly held beliefs or preferences. If you are a strict Creationist, read Richard Dawkins' *The Greatest Show on Earth: The Evidence for Evolution.* If you're a hardcore liberal democrat with socialist leanings, read *Atlas Shrugged* by Ayn Rand. If you're a libertarian, read Karl Marx and Frederic L. Bender's *The Communist Manifesto*. If you're squeamish, read any novel by Jack Ketchum or some of Stephen King's earlier works.

In short, read material that challenges how you think, jars your sensibilities, and puts your worldview on trial.

While reading, take copious notes, writing down or highlighting passages and ideas that you like or that may prove useful at some point. More importantly, pay careful attention to how the author structures the book, article, or story in question.

If you want to write mystery novels, for example, plow through a bunch of mystery novels. This is exactly what worked for Austin writer David Lindsey, author of the groundbreaking serial killer novel *Mercy* (1990), which was adapted for an HBO original movie in 2000.

According to Lindsey's website, he decided to "take the plunge" into writing novels in 1980, but he had a family to feed and a household to maintain, so he went the commercial route with popular fiction, specifically mysteries.

"Having never read a mystery novel," the website says, "Lindsey bought a representative collection of 25 popular, famous, and classic mystery novels, including European writers. After reading these, he realized that the genre encompassed a startling variety of work, everything from Mickey Spillane to Dostoyevsky."

To date, Lindsey is a full-time writer and has published 14 novels. The "read lots of books in your chosen genre" method may not let every prospective author quit his or her day job, but it's the best method I know of for learning how to write a novel.

In terms of world experience, it's important to get up from your couch or desk on a regular basis, meeting your neighbors, conversing with people of different backgrounds, and studying what they say and how they say it. Keep a pocket-sized notebook (or your iPhone or tablet) with you at all times, writing down (or typing) anything you hear that sounds interesting. This will help you write colorful sentences and create believable dialogue. It will also help spark ideas.

In addition to interacting with people, interact with your environment. Sit down in the park and write about everything you see and feel, describing the trees, the birds, the clouds, the wind, the rough texture of the wooden bench, the children at play, or anything else worthy of commenting on. This is a good exercise for helping you learn to write descriptive paragraphs.

Many writer wannabes view the art of writing as a mystical process in which it's only possible to write when you are inspired, either internally or by an outside source. Nothing could be further from the truth, at least in my experience (your mileage may vary—I can only tell you what I've discovered for myself).

While it's true that ideas will pop into your head from time to time from seemingly nowhere, and that characters you create can seem to take on a life of their own, the bottom line is that you have to sit your butt down every day for several hours and "just flail away at the goddamned thing" (to quote Stephen King). Without putting in days and weeks and months and years of hard work (which is oftentimes lonely, frustrating, and low paying, but which sometimes reaps huge rewards emotionally and financially), you, to put it bluntly, will probably never amount to anything as a writer.

That's not to say that writing can't be fun, and that it can't be an invigorating way to make a little extra money, but if you want to write for a living, you simply have to put in the work.

Or, as Ernest Hemingway once said, "There is nothing to writing. All you do is sit down at a typewriter and bleed."

How Writing Can Supplement Your Income

One of the hardest ways to make a living is to be a freelance writer. The odds of writing a best-seller, such as a blockbuster novel or a fad diet book that happens to catch fire, are astronomically small. Books that sell a few hundred or even a few thousand copies typically pay minimum wage or less, considering the time it takes to research and write a book. Moreover, unless your contract calls for a series of books, there's usually no guarantee that your next will book will get published. Self-publishing is an option, but these types of books (often called vanity projects) receive little publicity (i.e. whatever promotion you can provide) and rarely make much money for the author (though there are exceptions).

Syndicated columnists make good money, but relatively few writers are lucky or well-connected enough to obtain such a position. Joining the staff of a national magazine is a possibility, but relocating is usually a must, and these types of jobs are highly sought after, making the competition fierce. In addition, magazine staffers are often expected to have specialized computer skills that are outside of the purview (or interest level) of many freelancers. Writing screenplays is certainly profitable, but getting your script noticed usually requires Hollywood connections that most freelancers simply don't have. In short, well-paying writing gigs can be tough to come by.

While it's tough to support a family (or even yourself) solely by writing, freelance work can be a nice, creatively satisfying way to earn extra cash. If you are fresh off your first writing course or are otherwise new to the part-time profession of freelance writing, it's certainly okay to submit your articles and stories to non-paying markets, as getting published is good experience (not to mention good for the résumé) and a reward in and of itself. However, once you've been at it for a while and your work has the type of professional polish that editors are looking for (be sure and have friends or family read your work prior to sending it in), only submit your writing to paying markets. This may seem like a no-brainer, but writers often undervalue their hard work, settling for contributor copies and the thrill of seeing their name in print. Writing without getting paid is a hobby, not an occupation.

There are two schools of thought concerning what type of day job a freelance writer should have. Some writers like to engage in such professions as loading trucks, waiting tables, or repairing cars, all of which are noisily, jarringly different than writing. Other writers like to enmesh themselves in an academic environment, working as librarians, research assistants, or school teachers. A practical aspect of the more literary type of job is easy access to research materials and such tools as copier machines and computers. Regardless, your day job should complement, not take away from, your beloved writing.

Obviously, writers hoping to sell their work should consult various writers' markets, including such resources as Writer's Digest (www.writersdigest.com), Freelance Writing (www.freelancewriting.com), and Writers Weekly (www.writersweekly.com). Not only will you find magazines and electronic publications to submit your articles and stories to, you can garner story ideas by reading through the various guidelines. For example, a magazine may mention that they are looking for personal essays, such as childhood traumas. This could spark your memory of a particularly nasty event that, while certainly unpleasant, could be just the type of story the editor is looking for. And even if the story gets rejected by that editor, you can always submit it elsewhere. Just keep it in a file marked "nonfiction" or "unsold articles." (You do have a filing system, don't you?)

One of the most interesting and potential-filled markets today is Constant Content (www.constant-content.com), which lets writers post their articles for perspective clients to purchase. Writers edit their own work, but articles must be of professional quality or they'll be rejected. Writers can submit reprints (a good way to maximize profits on old articles that are just sitting around, collecting dust), but most buyers are looking for original material. Constant Content keeps 35% of the take, but there are no submission fees. If you've got an article that has been rejected repeatedly, or if you've got an article that you simply can't find a market for, Constant Content may be the way to go. Keep in mind that they don't accept fiction or poetry, nor will they consider articles told from a first-person perspective.

Regardless of your financial goals, write continuously, even when you seemingly have nothing to write about. Brainstorm, jot down stream-of-consciousness thoughts, write about your dog or cat, describe your best friend or your backyard, keep a daily journal, blog about the restaurant where you ate last night—anything to keep your butt in the chair and your fingers typing. And from those mad scribblings, you are sure to stumble across an idea or two for an article or a story. Plus, writing is a craft, and the more you do it, the better you will get. Moreover, you should read even more than you write.

It's not impossible to make a living as a writer, but most freelancers can't afford to quit their day job. What they can do is pocket extra spending money by getting published. And the key to getting published is to write, write, write, keeping the market in mind as you go, go, go.

*This article originally appeared in the April 23, 2012 issue of the *Fort Worth Star-Telegram*.

Writers in Movies

Mention Edgar Allan Poe to most anyone and they'll likely conjure up images of black ravens, tell-tale hearts, premature burials and haunted palaces. With "The Murders in the Rue Morgue" (1841), the short story writer, poet, editor and literary critic invented modern detective fiction, and his often-macabre work is still widely studied in schools today.

In *The Raven*, opening April 27, John Cusack plays the legendary author, who teams with a young Baltimore detective to investigate a series of crimes perpetrated by a serial killer using Poe's writings as inspiration. With this in mind, we thought it'd be fun to scare up a list of other films in which famous writers play prominent roles.

J.M. Barrie (1860–1937)
Finding Neverland (2004, PG)

Inspired by his friendship with the Davies boys, whom he later assumed guardianship of, J. M. Barrie created the ultimate fantasy in Peter Pan, a rambunctious boy who can fly and never grows up. Johnny Depp plays the Scottish novelist and playwright as a sincere, soft-spoken, highly imaginative, seemingly asexual man-child, playing games with the boys, making faces, dressing in silly costumes and wrestling with a large stuffed bear.

Depp as Barrie is believable and moving, and, despite his unconventional relationship with the Davies family, never seems creepy or inappropriate. Kate Winslet as the boys' mother, Sylvia Davies, complements Depp's performance nicely.

Truman Capote (1924–1984)

***Capote* (2005, Rated R)**

Best known for the novella *Breakfast at Tiffany's* (1958), which was made into a film starring Audrey Hepburn, and the "true crime novel" *In Cold Blood* (1966), which was adapted into three films and a TV mini-series, the diminutive, openly gay Truman Capote was also an acclaimed short story writer and a popular talk show guest.

Capote chronicles the writer's time researching and writing *In Cold Blood*, a project he poured himself into mind, body and (tortured) soul, interviewing police officers, the killers and neighbors of the murdered family. Philip Seymour Hoffman's uncanny portrayal of the toddler-voiced writer truly captures the quirky qualities that made Capote unique.

Ernest Hemingway (1899–1961)
***Midnight in Paris* (2011, PG-13)**

At the 2011 Cannes Film Festival press conference for *Midnight in Paris*, writer/director Woody Allen talked about his satirical characterizations of Ernest Hemingway, Salvador Dali and other Jazz Age writers and artists. "I wasn't trying to make them meaningful and deep and profound," he said. "I was just trying to make them amusing and entertaining."

As such, Corey Stoll is an egotistical, combative, hard-drinking caricature of Hemingway, speaking in bold, cinematic proclamations and challenging aspiring novelist Gil Pender (Owen Wilson) to a boxing match to determine who is the better writer. Hemingway, who revolutionized 20th century fiction with his terse, direct style, has never been so amusing.

C.S. Lewis (1898–1963)
***Shadowlands* (1993, Rated PG)**

Clive Staples Lewis was both a contemporary of fellow novelist J.R.R. Tolkien and a leading Christian apologist, penning such classics as *The Screwtape Letters*, *The Problem of Pain* and the "Chronicles of Narnia" fantasy series. He was also a distinguished professor at Oxford University.

Like the reputation of the man himself, *Shadowlands*, featuring the great Anthony Hopkins as Lewis, is quiet, understated, cerebral and contemplative. Romantic interest Joy Gresham, an American fan played beautifully by Deborah Winger, helps Lewis unbutton his buttoned-up life, making the dour dramatist shine in subtle and charming ways.

Dorothy Parker (1893–1967)
Mrs. Parker and the Vicious Circle (1994, Rated R)

The most famous member of the legendary Algonquin Round Table, which was a group of Roaring Twenties-era intellectuals that met regularly for lunch and recorded their verbal exploits in print, Dorothy Parker is remembered for her quick wit, caustic poetry, satirical short stories and fondness for alcohol. She was also quite beautiful.

Jennifer Jason Leigh's portrayal of Parker, who wrote for *Vanity Fair*, *The New Yorker* and other highbrow magazines, is sharp-tongued and knowingly smart and sexy, seducing the camera (she's clearly the centerpiece of the film), the other characters in the movie and, most importantly, the audience.

Beatrix Potter (1866–1943)
Miss Potter (2006, Rated PG)

Beatrix Potter, who plied her trade in Victorian England, was much more than the creator of such beloved children's books as *The Tale of Peter Rabbit* (1902), *The Tailor of Gloucester* (1903) and *Cecily Parsley's Nursery Rhymes* (1922). She also collected fossils, raised sheep, drew and painted bugs (entomology was one of her favorite areas of study) and actively participated in conservationism.

In *Miss Potter*, Renée Zellweger pours herself into the title role, giving viewers a quirky and likable author/illustrator to cheer for. Directed by Chris Noonan (*Babe*), the film includes brief animations that help Potter's unique artistic vision come alive.

Marquis de Sade (1740–1814)
Quills (2000, Rated R)

The infamous Marquis de Sade, writer of novels, plays, political tracts, short stories and violence-infused erotica, was a notorious hedonist, whoremonger and blasphemer (a serious crime 200+ years ago), living nearly one-third of his life locked in prisons and an insane asylum (today, he'd probably receive a star on the Hollywood Walk of Fame).

In *Quills*, Geoffrey Rush plays the licentious libertine during his still-sadistic (a term derived from de Sade's name) senior years at the famous Charenton asylum. Like most biopics, *Quills* plays fast and loose with history, but it's true that de Sade wrote much of his material while tucked safely away from polite society.

Jerry Stahl (1953–)
Permanent Midnight (1998, Rated R)

Jerry Stahl may not be a household name, but he's certainly had an imprint on popular culture, writing episodes of *ALF*, *Moonlighting*, *thirtysomething*, *Twin Peaks* and, most notably, *CSI* (including the controversial "King Baby" episode, which dealt with infantilism).

Permanent Midnight is based on Stahl's 2005 autobiography, which deals with the troubled writer's $6,000-a-week heroin habit (contrast this with his $5,000-per-week salary) and his tendency to be high during TV script conferences. Ben Stiller, primarily known for his comedic roles, plays Stahl convincingly, especially when it comes to getting across the miserable desperation of addiction and withdrawal.

Virginia Woolf (1882–1941)
The Hours (2002, PG-13)

Along with such intellectuals as economist John Maynard Keynes and novelist E.M. Forster, Virginia Woolf belonged to the Bloomsbury Set, a group of artistic types who got together on a regular basis in and around Bloomsbury, London, during the first half of the 20th century. An early feminist, Woolf is famous for writing the lengthy essay *A Room of One's Own* (1929), along with the novels *Mrs. Dalloway* (1925), *To the Lighthouse* (1927) and *Orlando* (1928).

In *The Hours*, a truly gloomy film, Nicole Kidman masterfully transforms herself literally (check out the bulbous nose) and figuratively into Woolf, who battled depression throughout her life, ultimately committing suicide. Kudos to Kidman for her willingness to be unattractive onscreen.

Ed Wood (1924–1978)
Ed Wood (1994, Rated R)

Like Orson Welles, Ed Wood wrote, directed, produced and acted in many of his films. Unlike Welles, however, Wood had little discernible talent, helming such so-bad-they're-entertaining bombs as *Glen or Glenda* (1953), *Bride of the Monster* (1955) and *Plan 9 from Outer Space* (1959), the latter of which was immortalized in an episode of *Seinfeld* ("The Chinese Restaurant"). Wood also penned a number of dreadful paperback originals, all of which are rare and highly sought after by collectors.

Tim Burton's *Ed Wood* is a marvelous film, with Johnny Depp absolutely nailing the title role of the eccentric, naively optimistic, angora-wearing auteur. Especially fun are the scenes reenacting some of Wood's more infamous movies.

*This article originally appeared in *AntiqueWeek*.

The History of Typewriters

Like the pedal-powered sewing machine, the mechanical calculator, and the CB radio, the typewriter is a remnant of the past, an outdated mechanism that has been replaced by a more efficient form of technology—in this case the home computer.

During the early 1980s, when such personal computers as the Apple II and the Commodore 64 were popular, people were undoubtedly intrigued by the futuristic seeming machines. However, techno geeks and modernists aside, most people scoffed at the notion that the majority of American households would one day contain at least one computer.

The reason for the skepticism was that older computers, at least in the average consumer's mind, did little more than play games, manage grocery lists, calculate numbers, host nerdy bulletin board sites, and process words (obviously, such popular applications as eBay, email, facebook, and the like were still years away).

Many secretaries, writers, and other typists of the era called computers "glorified word processors," and since word processors, which proliferated during the 1970s and '80s, were much cheaper than their more sophisticated counterparts, computers were often considered an expensive luxury item, not a necessity.

The main thing computers and word processors shared in common, other than their ability to process words via a human-controlled keyboard, is that they made the common typewriter—including the electric typewriter—obsolete. Some may pine for the days of the typewriter, but there's no doubting that computers (and word processors, which have basically been replaced by computers) make writing much easier.

With computers you can save your files, delete mistakes, rearrange sentences and paragraphs, print and email multiple copies of your work, and much, much more, all with a few button presses. Typewriters, on the other hand, are cumbersome and unwieldy. If you screw up while typing, you have to leave it as is, retype the entire page, correct the mistake with a typewriter eraser, or paint over the mistake with liquid paper, let it dry, and then retype over that section. Dry correction techniques were introduced in the 1970s, making the process easier, but still far less than ideal.

Clearly, computers make processing words faster and more convenient, but there are a few noteworthy authors who still use typewriters. Woody Allen, in a recent documentary broadcast on PBS, admitted that he writes his film scripts in longhand on a legal pad and then transcribes them with a typewriter.

Harlan Ellison, author of more than 1,700 short stories, essays, novellas, screenplays, and teleplays (including the acclaimed *Star Trek* episode "City on the Edge of Forever"), is no luddite, but he rails against the concept of using computers to make writing easier.

In an interview published on his website, Ellison Webderland (harlanellison.com), Ellison says, "Using PCs [personal computers] for doing term papers, or scientific treatises, for lists, for stuff like that, it's fine, but NOT for creative work."

Ellison claims that computers make people write in a more slovenly fashion. "They are not nearly as alert to the fact that they're going to actually have to do the physical labor of changing something," he says. "All they know is that if they do it wrong, all they have to do is press a button. What this means is that we have nothing but long, windy novels that are three times the length that they ought to be. We have trilogies and tetralogies that are idiotic, that are chewing the cud a million times over, and the only thing I've ever heard in aid of using a computer over a typewriter is it makes it easier."

In Ellison's mind, the word "easier" can be a pejorative. "Making it easier, I think, is invidious," he says. "It is a really BAD thing. Art is not supposed to be easier! There are a lot of things in life that *are* supposed to be easier. Ridding the world of heart attacks, making the roads smoother, making old people more comfortable in the winter, but not art. Art should always be tough. Art should demand something of you. Art should involve foot-pounds of energy being expended. It's not supposed to be easier, and those who want it easier should not be artists. They should be out selling public relations copy."

One drawback to using typewriters, Ellison admits, is that the technology is outdated, making equipment difficult to restock. "What offends me is that I can no longer find typewriter ribbons, that there is no one around that can repair my typewriter, that I've had to learn to do it myself...I will not be one of those people who loses the ability to tell time on a clock with hands because I've had digitals all my life. I will not be one of those M.I.T. students who cannot use a slipstick because I've got a little PC that will do it for me."

While Ellison still uses a typewriter in his work, he recently sold his first typewriter—a Remington noiseless portable. Ellison listed it for $40,000, and it sold to Jamie Ford, the New York Times best-selling author of *Hotel on the Corner of Bitter and Sweet*. On his blog, Ford says that Ellison's work made him want to be a writer, but that he "didn't pay anywhere *near* $40,000."

David Silver, who brokered the Ellison deal, says the pricing was "comparable" to the sale of Jack Kerouac's typewriter, a Hermes 3000 manual, which sold for $22,500. In stark contrast, Cormac McCarthy's typewriter, a Lettera 32 Olivetti manual, recently sold for $254,500. On the lower end, a typewriter that belonged to John Updike sold for $4,375. (McCarthy's typewriter sold in 2009, the others in 2010).

While computers have rendered typewriters largely unnecessary, there are certain functions that typewriters handle better, at least according to Chuck Dilts of the Early Typewriter Collectors' Association. "We have a collector friend in Rhode Island who is in charge of keeping a working typewriter at the office where he works," Dilts says. "Many people find it much easier to address an envelope with a typewriter rather than formatting it through the computer and printer. Also, forms that are used only occasionally, or those with multiple copies, are better done on a typewriter."

Dilts doesn't use a typewriter on a regular basis, but he, along with partner Rich Cincotta (co-publishers emeritus of *ETCetera, the Journal of the Early Typewriter Collectors Association*), collects them voraciously. At one point they owned more than 900 typewriters.

When asked about some of the more interesting typewriters in his collection, Dilts cited The Gardner, which uses only 14 keys to print all the characters. "You have to press one, two, sometimes three keys to get the desired character," he said.

Dilts also referenced The Child's Typewriter. "It looks like a toy, but it was sold as an inexpensive index-style typewriter," he said. "It's basically a wheel on a stick with a plate that sits on the paper. You put the wheel down at the character you want, roll it toward the hole in the plate, and it prints the character through a hole on the plate. Where you put the wheel down determines how far around it goes, therefore which character it prints."

Dilts declined to discuss the value of his collection, and he's skeptical of the pricing information found in the various collector books. However, he does recommend Darryl Rehr's *Antique Typewriters & Office Collectibles* (Collector Books, 1997) as a "good field guide." *Antique Typewriters & Office Collectibles* is readily available on Amazon.com, but Rehr's other book, *The Early History of the Typewriter*, (Rehr, 1997), is hard to find.

The concept of writing machines dates back to at least 1714, when a patent was filed in England by Henry Mill for such a device. In 1808, an Italian named Pelligrino Turri developed a machine that enabled the blind to write letters to sighted persons (Turri also devised carbon paper to provide ink for his invention).

In 1829, William Austin Burt patented the typographer, which some sources cite as the first typewriter. The first commercially produced typewriter was the Hansen Writing Ball, which was invented by Danish minster Rasmus Malling-Hansen in 1865 and first produced in 1870.

According to the Early Office Museum (www.officemuseum.com), "The first typewriter that enabled operators to write significantly faster than a person could write by hand was the Sholes & Glidden Type Writer, which was introduced in 1874 by E. Remington & Sons." This early machine used the QWERTY keyboard, but typed only in capital letters. A later model allowed for both upper and lowercase letters.

The first commercially successful typewriter was the Remington 2, which hit stores in 1878.

Early typewriters, like so many other outdated devices, have gone up in value in recent years as baby boomers, nostalgia buffs, and other collectors clamor to get their hands on a piece of history. A recent search of completed eBay auctions turned up the following prices on vintage typewriters:

1906 Smith Premiere No. 2 with case: $725
1932 Woodstock No. 5: $600 (plus $57.15 shipping)
1937 Remington No. 5 refurbished: $499.95

1937 Royal Model O with case: $355 (plus $23.11 shipping)
1967 Yellow Royal Safari: $349.95 (plus $27.64 shipping)
1973 Blue Hermes 3000 refurbished: $349.95
1973 Olivetti Lettera 31 refurbished: $299.95.
1939 Maroon Smith Corona: $275
1917 Underwood Model No. 5: $229
1913 Hammond Multiplex with curved keyboard: $850

When bidding on an old typewriter, potential buyers should carefully check the seller's description. Many vintage typewriters have missing keys or keys that simply don't function.

Luckily, if the typewriter you purchase doesn't work, you can always fall back on that most ubiquitous of items: the computer.

Or, if you are really old-fashioned, the word processor.

Interview with Author James Reasoner

Often cranking out more than a million words in a single year, James Reasoner, who is married to author Livia Washburn-Reasoner, is one of the most prolific writers on the planet. He's had more than 300 novels published (under his own name and under various pseudonyms), along with more than 100 short stories. Like the pulp fiction writers of old, Reasoner is a genre specialist, writing mysteries (including *Texas Wind*, the first private eye novel set in Fort Worth), fantasy stories, adventure yarns, historical dramas and, most prominently, tales of the Old West.

I conducted this interview with Mr. Reasoner a few years ago.

BRETT WEISS: Where did you and your wife grow up, and what was it like?

JAMES REASONER: Both of us grew up in Azle, Texas and went all the way through school here. The town was much smaller in the fifties and sixties, and there was a feeling of knowing everybody in town, even though of course we didn't. But I knew a lot of people, because my father was a television repairman and had customers all over the area. Azle was a very friendly, comfortable place to grow up.

WEISS: Where and how did you meet?

REASONER: Livia's older brother Bruce and I were in the same first-grade class and were friends all the way through school, so I've known the Washburn family practically all my life. I never really got to know Livia that well until I was college, though. Her brother and I drove to Denton together every day to attend what was then North Texas State University, so I started talking to Livia when I would get to their house and have to wait for Bruce.

WEISS: What made you want to be a writer?

REASONER: I got hooked on books and reading when I was six–years-old. A bookmobile used to come out to Azle every Saturday from the Fort Worth Public Library and park under a shade tree on Main Street. My sister took me to check out books one Saturday, and I was never the same after that. I always made up stories for my own enjoyment and started writing them down when I was in fifth grade. I wanted to be a writer and started submitting stories to magazines when I was in college. I wasn't able to sell any of them and had almost given up on it by the time I had graduated and gotten married. Livia encouraged me to keep trying, and within a few months I began to sell a few stories here and there. I've been at it ever since.

WEISS: Describe, if you would, what it was like when your house burned down.

REASONER: I was home alone that morning, sitting in the living room with my laptop, working on a book. We knew it was a Red Flag Warning day, so I noticed right away when I began to smell smoke. I ran outside and saw that the entire field behind our house was on fire, about 400 yards wide, and coming straight at our house with a 50-mile-per-hour wind behind it. I actually grabbed the water hose, thinking that I was going to fight it, then realized I wouldn't have any chance to stop it. I ran inside, grabbed our little dog who was recuperating from surgery at the time, and got out. There were thick clouds of smoke all around, but we managed to stay where we could breathe and finally worked our way across some fences and through some fields to another road. I was able to get in touch with Livia, and we met up about half a mile away from the house, but by then we couldn't get back into the area because the roads were closed. It was late that afternoon before we were able to get to the house and see that it had burned to the ground.

WEISS: What did you lose in the fire (manuscripts, published work, pets, and anything else you want to add), and what were you able to save?

REASONER: We lost three cats, a bird, and a dwarf goat. Our other dog got out of the front yard and escaped on his own. All our manuscripts and published work were gone, along with all the family photos and things from our daughters' childhood, plus tens of thousands of books I'd collected over the past forty years. When I went back in the house while the fire was practically on top of it, I grabbed the dog, but not my laptop, which means I lost everything I had done on the book I was writing, which amounted to about half of it. That night we stayed with my wife's parents, and in the middle of the night I was up making notes, putting down everything I could remember about the book so I could recreate it. We both had contracts and deadlines and couldn't afford not to keep writing, so within a couple of days we had new computers and tried to carry on as best we could.

WEISS: What have you guys been doing this past year, and what writing projects are you working on now?

REASONER: We figured out pretty quickly that we wanted to rebuild in the same place, so we managed to move a mobile home onto the property to live in while we were working on that. Our writing slowed down for about a month (but never stopped completely), and since then it's been back to its regular pace. I've been writing Westerns, historical novels, and thrillers under several different pseudonyms, and I'm working on a Western series that will be published under my name. Last year I wrote the first novel in the "Gabriel Hunt" adventure series, which received starred reviews from *Publishers Weekly* and *Booklist* and made *Publishers Weekly*'s list of the Top 100 Books published in 2009. I've also had several books under pseudonyms make the *USA Today* and *New York Times* bestseller lists in the past couple of years.

WEISS: What's it like starting over?

REASONER: It's the roughest thing I've ever done. Luckily, we had plenty of friends and family who helped us in every way imaginable—money, household goods, furniture, family photos, etc. Also, people from all over the world donated books to help us rebuild our library. The outpouring of love and support was phenomenal, and we couldn't have made it without everyone who helped.

WEISS: Are you in a new house now? If so, did you have it built yourselves?

REASONER: Yes, the fire took place on January 29, 2008, and by December of that year we were able to move into a beautiful new house built by a couple of friends of ours from school, Larry and Karen Mackey, who are great contractors.

WEISS: What are your writing schedules like? Do you have your own separate offices, or do you work side by side? Do you take breaks together?

REASONER: We have separate offices. Mine is in the bonus room over our garage, so we're even on different floors. I've never been a "work every day" sort of writer, but I write five or six days a week, usually from about nine o'clock in the morning until six in the evening, with a break for lunch. I can do more than that if I have to, but not day in and day out. Livia's schedule is more hectic than mine, so some days we don't see each other much, even though we both work at home.

WEISS: How has the fire changed your attitude towards work and life in general?

REASONER: I think seeing how everything can vanish in a matter of minutes has made me more appreciative of the good things in life, and it's certainly made me appreciate my family and friends even more than I did before. Work really helped me keep my sanity. What happened was terrible, but I didn't have time to sit around and brood about it. I had books I had to get written. The day of the fire, I went to the library here in Azle to use one of their computers and email my main editor to let him know what had happened. I told him about losing the book I was working on for him and said that if he wanted to get someone else to take over some of my contracts, I understood. He emailed back the next day and said that he would drive nails through his hands before he would let anybody take any books away from me. When people have that much faith in you, you can't let them down.

*Chris Cavanaugh of *Classic Gamer Magazine* interviewed me back in 2009. Here's the result:

Interview with Brett Weiss

Pop culture expert Brett Weiss has written numerous articles that have appeared in the *Comics Buyer's Guide, Fangoria,* Allgame.com, and past issues of *Classic Gamer Magazine.* Brett recently authored two books: *Classic Home Video Games: 1972-1984* and *Classic Home Video Games: 1985-1988* and agreed to talk to us about the challenges of writing, getting published, and how mowing lawns is good for the game collector's soul.

CLASSIC GAMER MAGAZINE: Convincing a major book publisher to publish a book isn't easy. Can you tell us how the initial deal happened? Did you approach them or was it the other way around?

BRETT WEISS: McFarland Publishers, which publishes a variety of scholarly entertainment books, had a booth at Comic-Con International in San Diego in 2006, and I introduced myself to one of their editors. I gave her a business card and told her to contact me if I could contribute to any of their books. Three days after I returned home, I received an email from that editor, asking me if I had any interesting book ideas.

I quickly pounded out a proposal and some sample entries, emphasizing that a book like mine had never been done before: descriptions/reviews/data for every single game for every U.S.-released classic programmable system. They approved the idea pretty quickly.

During the early-to mid-1990s, I worked up a proposal for a similar book, but I couldn't find a publisher.

CGM: How much influence does the publisher have on content? Did you have to make sacrifices?

WEISS: The publisher was very receptive to my original proposal, and both books are pretty much exactly like I conceived and wrote them. During the editors' meeting, my proposal was approved unanimously. They loved the nostalgic content, the quality of the writing, and the comprehensive nature of the books. The only sticking point was their insistence on spelling the word "videogame" as two words.

CGM: What are the challenges associated with writing these books?

WEISS: Condensing a long RPG or point-and-click adventure down to a clear and concise, yet detailed overview. Trudging through horrible games. Getting far enough into really hard games to describe and review them accurately and fairly. The sheer exhaustion of having to write about the games in addition to playing them. Not having enough time to play new games because I'm so busy with the old systems.

Luckily, I largely prefer older games, but I'd love to have enough time and energy to pick up a PS3 and play through *God of War III* and *Batman: Arkham Asylum*. On the other hand, I love discovering obscure gems that I had never played before, such as the wildly inventive and hugely entertaining *Killer Bees!* for the Odyssey2. That was the last game I wrote about for my first book—I had to buy the game on eBay.

CGM: What was their reasoning for wanting to release the books in hardcover? Did you try to convince them otherwise? Do you think the decision has helped or hurt sales?

WEISS: I had absolutely no say in the matter. I was flattered that the books were published in hardcover, but I have met resistance by some potential buyers because of the hardcover pricing. On the other hand, everyone I've talked to who has bought either book is very happy with their purchase(s). People tell me they refer to my books again and again, and that's the best compliment I could ever get. I'm also frequently told that the books are well-written, which is always good to hear.

CGM: Is there talk about making these books available in paperback?

WEISS: Nothing yet, but hopefully some day. (NOTE: *Classic Home Video Games, 1972-1984* and *Classic Home Video Games, 1985-1988* have since come out in softcover).

CGM: What percentage of research goes into your books vs. how much you just know off the top of your head?

WEISS: I wouldn't quite say that the books wrote themselves, but I have been playing these games nonstop since they came out. The first system I actually owned was a ColecoVision when I was 15, but prior to the release of the ColecoVision, I was constantly going over to friends' and relatives' houses to play their systems. In fact, my two best friends each had a Fairchild Channel F of all things.

After I got my ColecoVision for Christmas of 1982 (I actually had to kick in $100 of my lawn mowing money to make it happen), I began collecting games like crazy (my second system was an Atari 2600 with 10 games that I bought off a classmate for the incredibly low price of $10).

I would get new systems as they would come out, but I never got rid of my older systems. I simply kept adding to them as I would find older games on clearance and at garage sales, flea markets, and thrift stores. Despite my familiarity with old games, I still do tons of research to make sure I get everything as accurate as possible, and to refresh my memory for games I haven't played in a long time.

CGM: Do you use any magazines or websites for research? Which ones?

WEISS: Thanks to their instruction manual scans, AtariAge and Nintendo Age were absolutely invaluable when I was writing my first two books. As everyone knows, it's much tougher to find manuals than game cartridges. I also used gamefaqs walkthroughs a few times when I had trouble getting past a certain area or level in a particularly hard or confusing game.

Digital Press has been helpful as well. When a game's manual or title screen doesn't mention who the developer is, and when various websites have conflicting information, I sometimes ask on the Digital Press message boards, and I usually get a response. Of course, I will then do more research to determine if the information they gave me is accurate.

CGM: Just to get inside your head a little bit, can you tell us about what goes into your writing process?

WEISS: I play the games in the evening and wake up early the next morning--oftentimes as early as 3 or 4 a.m.—to write about them. Prior to sitting down to my desk, I'll fire up a steaming hot cup of Earl Grey tea. I tried Earl Grey back when Captain Picard would order it from the food replicator on *Star Trek: The Next Generation* (yes, I'm a geek), and quickly became addicted to it.

I've been a freelance writer for almost 20 years, so I've got a pretty good routine in place. Comfortable pants/shorts and a good, sturdy chair that supports the back are absolutely essential. I write most every morning (and most afternoons), but I sometimes take Saturday morning off if my kids get up when I do.

CGM: How long did it take to write each of the books?

WEISS: The first book took about a year. *Classic Home Video Games, 1985-1988* took over two years, partly because most of the games from that era are longer and more complex.

CGM: How has the feedback been from those who've purchased the books? Have there been any interesting suggestions?

WEISS: The feedback has largely been terrific. Both books have reviewed extremely well. The most frequent comment I get is that people use the books when they are looking to purchase some older games they may enjoy. This is followed closely by people using the books because they can't remember a specific fact about a particular game, or just because they're fun to flip through. Some readers comment that they wish the photos were in color, but that is entirely up to the publisher.

CGM: Approximately how many copies have the books sold?
WEISS: I would tell you, but then I'd have to kill you. I can tell you that the first book has almost sold through its first printing, which is nice. With the new book, it's too early to tell.

CGM: What era of gaming do you enjoy most and why?

WEISS: While I've had a truly great time with such titles as *Halo*, *God of War*, *Wii Sports*, and *Burnout*, my favorite games are from the late '70s and early '80s. Games like *Dig Dug*, *Galaga*, *Super Pac-Man*, *Zoo Keeper* and *Phoenix* are simple, but challenging, intense, strategic, and endlessly replayable. *Mr. Do!* is my all-time favorite game. I still keep records of my highest scores on many of my favorite old games (again, the geek factor rears its ugly head).

CGM: In another interview, you said that your favorite platform was the ColecoVision. Of all the platforms you've written about, what makes the ColecoVision so special in your eyes?

WEISS: I love how Coleco took such second (and third) tier arcade games as *Frenzy*, *Carnival*, *Lady Bug*, *Pepper II*, *Space Panic*, *Slither*, and *Mouse Trap*, emulated them beautifully, and made them available for home play. These were great games that were unfairly overlooked until they made it into gamers' living rooms. Since you could play the games again and again without having to put in a quarter every time, you could take the time to truly discover how great these games were. Plus, there are great third-party titles like *Jumpman Junior* and *Miner 2049'er*. Some complain about the controllers, but I like them.

My favorite modern system is the PS2, partly because of its many arcade classics collections, but also because of some great modern games like *Lumines*, *REZ*, and *Maximo: Ghosts to Glory*.

CGM: Can you tell us anything about the third book you are currently writing?

WEISS: Absolutely! It will cover the Genesis, Neo Geo, and TurboGrafx-16. Hopefully, it will be out some time in mid-late 2011. (NOTE: *Classic Home Video Games, 1989-1990: A Complete Guide to Sega Genesis, Neo Geo and TurboGrafx-16 Games* was published in Aug. of 2011).

About the Author

A lifelong fan of comic books, video games, movies, science fiction, and the like, Brett Weiss has published professionally since 1997 and today is a full-time freelance writer.

Weiss is the author of six books: *The 100 Greatest Console Video Games: 1977-1987* (Schiffer, 2014); *Retro Pop Culture A to Z: From Atari 2600 to Zombie Films* (CreateSpace, 2013); *Classic Home Video Games 1972-1984* (McFarland, 2007); *Classic Home Video Games 1985-1988* (McFarland, 2009); *Classic Home Video Games 1989-1990* (McFarland, 2011); and *How to Get Published: 50 Successful Query Letters* (CreateSpace, 2014).

In addition, Weiss has had articles published in the *Fort Worth Star-Telegram*, *The Writer*, *Mystery Scene*, *AntiqueWeek*, *Antique Trader*, *Fangoria*, *Filmfax*, *Game Informer*, *Video Game Trader*, *Classic Gamer Magazine*, the *Comics Buyer's Guide*, *Toy Shop*, *Toy Cars & Models*, *Back Issue*, *Alter Ego*, *Robot*, *Native Peoples*, and various other publications. He's also been honored by video game legend Walter Day with four cards in Day's Twin Galaxies trading card set.

When not writing, Weiss enjoys reading, hiking, cycling, playing basketball and tennis, watching movies, going to museums, collecting video games, and hanging out with his family.

Weiss lives in Fort Worth, Texas with his lovely wife, who is essential in helping him with various computer and photography conundrums that frequently arise; his two wonderful kids, who do a great job of making life fun; and two crazy dogs and a fat cat.